W9-CLC-468

DISCOVERING CAREERS FOR YOUR FUTURE

radio &
television

Ferguson
An imprint of ☑®Facts On File

Ferguson
An imprint of Facts On File, Inc.
132 West 31st Street
New York NY 10001

Discovering careers for your future: radio & television.
  p. cm.
Includes bibliographical references and index.
  ISBN 0-8160-5846-6 (hc : alk. paper)
  1. Broadcasting—Vocational guidance.
  PN1990.55.D57 2005
  384.54'023'73—dc22   2004012838

Ferguson books are available at special discounts when purchased in bulk
quantities for businesses, associations, institutions, or sales promotions.
Please call our Special Sales Department in New York at (212) 967-8800 or
(800) 322-8755.

You can find Ferguson on the World Wide Web at http://www.fergpubco.com

Text design by Mary Susan Ryan-Flynn

Printed in the United States of America

EB FOF 10 9 8 7 6 5 4 3 2

This book is printed on acid-free paper.

Contents

Introduction

Y ou may not have decided yet what you want to be in the future. And you do not have to decide right away. You do know that right now you are interested in radio and television. Do any of the statements below describe you? If so, you may want to begin thinking about what a career in radio and television might mean for you.

___I enjoy performing in front of an audience.

___I like to make movies with my video camera.

___I enjoy putting on plays with my friends.

___I like to use my hands to make or build things.

___I like to write songs, plays, or stories.

___I like to listen to or record sounds and music.

___I watch as many television shows as I can.

___I enjoy watching, listening to, and talking about sports.

___I enjoy listening to the radio.

___I enjoy photography.

___I spend a lot of time using art, illustration, or video-editing programs on my computer.

___I like to discover new music, television shows, or books and tell my friends about them.

___I am fascinated by the weather.

Discovering Careers for Your Future: Radio & Television is a book about careers in radio and television, from actors to disc jockeys to television directors. Careers in this field can be found in television studios, radio stations, sports stadiums, recording studios, business offices, and production houses. While the television industry is centered in Los Angeles and New York, television and radio workers are employed in most major cities in the United States and throughout the world.

This book describes many careers in radio and television. Read through it and see how the different careers are connected. For example, if you are interested in working in front of the camera or microphone, you should read the articles on actors, disc jockeys, reporters, and sports broadcasters and announcers. If you are interested in working behind the scenes in a creative position, you will want to read about screenwriters, television directors, television editors, and other careers. If your interests are more technical in nature, you will want to read about audio recording engineers, broadcast engineers, lighting technicians, and other careers.

What Do Radio and Television Workers Do?

The first section of each chapter begins with a heading such as "What Television Producers Do" or "What Real-Time Captioners Do." This section tells what it is like to work at this job. It describes typical responsibilities and assignments. You will find out about working conditions. Which workers are employed on television sets? Which ones work at computers in offices? Which ones work in newsrooms? This section answers these and other questions.

How Do I Become a Radio or Television Worker?

The section called "Education and Training" describes the level of schooling you need for employment in each job—a high school diploma, training at a junior college, a college degree, or more. It also talks about on-the-job training that you can expect to receive after you are hired, and whether or not you must complete an apprenticeship program.

How Much Do Radio and Television Workers Earn?

The "Earnings" section gives salary figures for the job described in the chapter. These figures give you a general idea of how much money people with this job can make. Keep in mind that many people really earn more or less than the amounts given here because actual salaries depend on many different things, such as the size of the company, the location of the company, and the amount of education, training, and experience you have. Generally, but not always, bigger companies located in major cities pay more than smaller ones in smaller cities and towns, and people with more education, training, and experience earn more. Also remember that these figures are current or recent salaries. They will probably be different by the time you are ready to enter the workforce.

What Is the Future of Radio and Television Careers?

The "Outlook" section discusses the employment outlook for the career: whether the total number of people employed in this career will increase or decrease in the coming years and whether jobs in this field will be easy or hard to find. These predictions are based on economic conditions, the size and makeup of the population, foreign competition, and new technology. Terms such as "faster than the average," "about as fast as the average," and "slower than the average" are used by the U.S. Department of Labor to describe job-growth predictions.

Keep in mind that these predictions are general statements. No one knows for sure what the future will be like. Also remember that the employment outlook is a general statement about an industry and does not necessarily apply to everyone. A determined and talented person may be able to find a job in an industry or career with the worst outlook. And a person without ambition and the proper training will find it difficult to find a job in even a booming industry or career field.

Where Can I Find More Information?

Each chapter concludes with a "For More Info" section. It lists resources that you can contact to find out more about the field and careers in the field. You will find the names, addresses, phone numbers, and websites of radio and television associations and organizations.

Extras

Every chapter has a few extras. There are photos that show radio and television workers in action. There are sidebars and notes on ways to explore the field, fun facts, profiles of people in the field, or lists of websites and books that might be helpful. At the end of the book you will find a Browse and Learn More section, a glossary, and an index. The Browse and Learn More section lists general radio and television books and websites to explore. The glossary gives brief definitions of words that relate to education, career training, or employment that you may be unfamiliar with. The index includes all the job titles mentioned in the book.

It is not too soon to think about your future. We hope you discover several possible career choices in the radio and television industries. Have fun exploring!

Actors

What Actors Do

Actors perform in stage plays, television and movies, videos, and radio productions. They use voice, movement, and gestures to portray different characters. Actors spend a lot of time looking for available parts. They read and study the parts and then audition for the director and producers of the show. In television and film, actors must also do screen tests, which are scenes recorded on videotape or film. Once selected for a role, actors memorize their lines and rehearse with other cast members. Rehearsal times are usually longer for live theater performances than for television and film productions. If the production includes singing and dancing, it requires more rehearsal time.

Television actors in a series, such as a soap opera or a situation comedy, may play the same role for years, generally in 13-week cycles. For these actors, however, their lines change from week to week and even from day to day, and much time is spent rehearsing new lines. Other television actors perform in made-for-TV movies, commercials, music videos, and documentaries. Television actors usually perform scenes out of

Study with the Masters

For over 50 years, The Actors Studio has taught the "method" style of acting to some of the greatest actors. Method acting was developed from the work of Konstantin Stanislavsky of Russia, and was taught by Lee Strasberg. It was made famous by Marlon Brando, Dustin Hoffman, Robert DeNiro, and many others.

The Actors Studio now has a master of fine arts degree program at the New School University in New York. The three-year program was created by studio members James Lipton, Paul Newman, Ellen Burstyn, Arthur Penn, Norman Mailer, Carlin Glynn, Lee Grant, and Peter Masterson.

Visit the Actors Studio website at http://www.newschool.edu/academic/drama.

EXPLORING

○ Participate in school or community theater productions. You can audition for acting roles, but also work on costumes, props, or lighting to get theater experience.

○ Watch as many television shows, movies, and plays as you can.

○ Read biographies of famous actors and other books about acting, auditioning, theater, and the television, radio, and film industries. You can also find biographies of actors on A&E Television Network website http://www.biography.com.

sequence during filming—they may perform the last scene first, for example. They also may have to repeat the same scene many times. *Radio actors* perform in comedies, dramas, documentaries, and in other radio programming. Unlike other actors who are seen on film or videotape, radio actors can only use their voices to convey emotion or tell a story.

Acting is often seen as a glamorous profession, yet many actors work long and irregular hours for both rehearsals and performances, often at low wages. Actors must frequently travel to work in different theaters and on location.

Education and Training

Besides natural talent, actors need determination, a good memory, a fine speaking voice, and, if possible, the ability to sing and dance. Actors who appear in musicals usually have studied singing and dancing for years in addition to their training in drama.

Although it is not required, a college education is helpful. High school and community theaters offer acting opportunities, and large cities such as New York, Chicago, and Los Angeles have public high schools for the performing arts. Special dramatic arts schools, located mainly in New York and Los Angeles, also offer training.

Earnings

The wage scale for actors and actresses is set by actors' unions. In 2003, the minimum daily salary of any member of the

Screen Acting and Stage Acting

Screen acting differs from acting in a theater. In screen work, the camera can focus closely on an actor, so performances must be subtle and lifelike. Stage work requires more exaggerated gestures and speaking techniques. Film and television actors spend a lot of time waiting for scenes to be filmed. They repeat the same scene over and over, play scenes out of order, and perform only small segments of a scene at a time. Stage actors perform an entire play at one time. Unless they work in front of a live audience, screen actors do not receive an audience reaction until months after they perform. Stage actors get an immediate reaction from the audience while they are performing.

Screen Actors Guild (SAG) in a speaking role was $678, or $2,352 for a five-day workweek. Motion picture actors may also receive additional payments known as residuals as part of their guaranteed earnings. Many motion picture actors receive residuals whenever films, TV shows, and TV commercials in which they appear are rerun, sold for TV exhibition, or released on DVD. Residuals often exceed the actors' original salary and account for about one-third of all actors' income.

According to the U.S. Department of Labor, the median yearly salary for all actors was $23,470 in 2002. The department also reported the lowest paid 10 percent earned less than $13,330 annually, while the highest paid 10 percent made more than $106,630.

In all areas of acting, well-known performers have salary rates above the minimums, and the salaries of top stars are many times higher. Actors in television series may earn tens of thousands of dollars per week, while a few may earn as much as $1 million or more per week. In film, top stars may earn as much as $20 million per film, and, after receiving a percentage

FOR MORE INFO

This union represents television and radio performers, including actors, announcers, dancers, disc jockeys, newspersons, singers, specialty acts, sportscasters, and stuntpersons.

American Federation of Television and Radio Artists
260 Madison Avenue
New York, NY 10016
Tel: 212-532-0800
Email: info@aftra.com
http://www.aftra.org

This union represents film and television performers. It has general information on actors, directors, and producers.

Screen Actors Guild
5757 Wilshire Boulevard
Los Angeles, CA 90036-3600
Tel: 213-549-6400
http://www.sag.org

This site has information for beginners on acting and the acting business.

Acting Workshop On-Line
http://www.redbirdstudio.com/AWOL/acting2.html

of the gross earned by the film, these stars can earn far, far more.

Outlook

Jobs in acting will grow about as fast as the average during the next decade, but acting is an overcrowded field. There always will be many more actors than there are roles to play. Cable television programming continues to add new acting opportunities. Many actors also work as secretaries, waiters, taxi drivers, or in other jobs to earn extra income.

Announcers

What Announcers Do

Announcers read the names and call letters of stations, announce station breaks, introduce and close shows, and make public service announcements. *Radio announcers* interview guests or moderate panel discussions. In some smaller stations, they are also responsible for keeping the station log, running the transmitter, and writing news and other scripts. *Television announcers* may report, present, and comment on the news or simply introduce network and news service reports.

Announcers have many specialized roles. For example, *disc jockeys* play music interspersed with commercial messages and talk. They sometimes read the news, weather forecasts, and traffic reports. Except for advertisements and news reports, most of their talk is unscripted and conversational. Disc jockeys can become quite popular; a few have even become national celebrities.

Sportscasters cover sports events for radio and television audiences. They have specialized knowledge of the sporting events they cover and are able to announce quickly and accurately what is happening during the event. Fast-moving sports such as hockey and basketball require a sportscaster who can describe the important events rapidly and without confusion.

To Be a Successful Announcer, You Should . . .

- have a pleasing voice and personality
- be levelheaded and able to speak calmly on the air
- have good diction and thorough knowledge of correct pronunciation
- dress professionally, especially if you are on television
- have a combination of sincerity and showmanship to attract a loyal audience

A radio announcer reads copy. (Corbis)

Newscasters specialize in reporting the news, including regional, national, and international events. Some newscasters also provide editorial commentary and personal opinions on news events and issues. In some instances, newscasters write their own scripts based on facts that are furnished by international news bureaus and other sources. In other instances, they read text exactly as it comes in. They may make as few as one or two reports each day if they work on a major news program, or they may broadcast news for five minutes every hour or half-hour. Newscasters may specialize in certain aspects of the news, such as economics, politics, health and medicine, or military activity.

News anchors are the primary announcers for half-hour or hour-long news programs and special news coverage. They read the main news events and then introduce reporters

EXPLORING

○ Write and record your own news report on audio or videotape. Critique your performance and keep practicing until you improve your delivery.

○ Practice your public speaking skills by joining a speech, debate, or forensics club.

○ Take tours of local radio and television stations.

○ Try to get a summer job at a radio or television station in your community.

who give more detailed coverage, including interviews and film clips.

Education and Training

To prepare for this career, take courses in English, communications, speech, and debate, as well as classes in radio and television techniques. Courses that offer vocal training are also helpful. A broad education will give you background knowledge and enable you to comment on national and world events and situations.

Most large radio and television stations prefer to hire announcers who have a bachelor's degree. Some trade schools offer programs in radio and television announcing, but you should investigate programs thoroughly before you enroll. Some of these programs are expensive and may offer little valuable training. You might talk to local radio or television station managers to get their opinions on which programs will be helpful and which ones to avoid.

Broadcast announcing is a highly competitive field. Although education and training requirements vary by employer, station officials pay particular attention to taped auditions and, in the case of television, to videotaped demos of sample presentations.

Books to Read

Esposito, Janet E. *In the SpotLight: Overcome Your Fear of Public Speaking and Performing.* Strong Books, 2000.

Keith, Michael C. *The Radio Station.* Burlington, Mass.: Focal Press, 2003.

Reese, David E., Mary E. Beadle, and Alan Stephenson. *Broadcast Announcing Worktext: Performing for Radio, Television, and Cable.* Burlington, Mass.: Focal Press, 2000.

FOR MORE INFO

For information about broadcast education and the broadcasting industry, contact
Broadcast Education Association
1771 N Street, NW
Washington, DC 20036-2891
Tel: 202-429-5354
Email: beainfo@beaweb.org
http://www.beaweb.org

To read answers to frequently asked questions about broadcasting, visit the NAB website.
National Association of Broadcasters (NAB)
1771 N Street, NW
Washington, DC 20036-2891
Tel: 202-429-5300
Email: nab@nab.org
http://www.nab.org

For industry information, contact
Radio-Television News Directors Association
1600 K Street, NW, Suite 700
Washington, DC 20006-2838
Tel: 202-659-6510
Email: rtnda@rtnda.org
http://www.rtnda.org

For career information and an overview of the industry, visit
About.com: Radio
http://radio.about.com

Earnings

According to a salary survey by the Radio-Television News Directors Association, announcers earn a wide range of salaries. Radio announcers earn a median salary of $22,000 with a low of $12,000 and a high of $45,000 or more. Television reporters and announcers earn a median salary of $26,000 with a low of $17,000 and a high of $300,000 or more.

Outlook

Competition for entry-level employment in announcing during the coming years is expected to be strong. There is a better chance of working in radio than in television because there are more radio stations. Local television stations usually carry a high percentage of network programs and need only a very small staff to carry out local operations. The top television markets are New York, Los Angeles, Chicago, Philadelphia, and San Francisco-Oakland-San Jose.

The number of new radio and television stations is growing slowly (if at all) due to industry consolidation. Thus, most openings will result from people leaving the industry or the labor force. Announcers who specialize in such areas as business, consumer, and health news should have an advantage over other job applicants.

Audio Recording Engineers

What Audio Recording Engineers Do

Audio recording engineers operate and maintain sound equipment used during musical recordings, film production, and radio and television broadcasts. When monitoring the sound of a project, engineers use master console boards with many switches, dials, and meters. Sound levels must be read and adjusted as a recording is being made. As recording technology has advanced, the work of audio recording engineers has had a larger effect on the sound of the final recorded product.

Audio recording engineers who work in the television and motion picture industries supervise all sounds that are created during a production. They test microphones, chords, recording equipment, and amplifiers to ensure that dialogue, sounds, special effects, and music are recorded correctly. They load tape players, set recording levels, and position microphones. Audio recording engineers often travel to shooting locations to set up and run sound equipment. They may work long hours on location and in the studio until a television show or film is completed.

Audio recording engineers are assisted in the studio by *sound mixers*.

Websites to Visit

Broadcast Engineering
http://www.broadcastengineering.com

Mix Magazine Online
http://mixonline.com

Pro Sound News
http://www.prosoundnews.com

Remix
http://www.remixmag.com

These technicians monitor the sound quality of audio recordings. They use much of the same sound recording equipment and control panels to assist the audio recording engineer.

Audio recording engineers frequently perform maintenance and repair on their equipment. They must identify and solve common technical problems in the studio or on location.

Being a recording engineer requires both technical skills and communication skills. Engineers must be patient, be capable of working well with a variety of people, and possess the confidence to function in a leadership position. Excellent troubleshooting skills are essential for success in this career.

Education and Training

During high school, take music courses to learn an instrument and learn music composition. You should also take classes in computer science and mathematics to prepare for the technical aspects of the career.

You'll need a high school diploma and at least two years of further training at a community college or technical school to become a recording engineer. You will need to earn an advanced degree if you are interested in becoming a supervisor. While new engineers receive on-the-job training in station procedures, they are expected to know the basics of broadcast technology before they are hired.

Most engineers interested in breaking into the film, radio, or television industries begin their careers performing a variety of tasks for smaller studios or stations. As engineers gain experience and skill, they

EXPLORING

○ If your school has a media department, learn how to work with some of its basic equipment.
○ Join a music or theater club to work in a sound booth during a live production.
○ Write or call record companies, recording studios, television studios, or motion picture studios to get more information.
○ Read books and music trade magazines that cover sound production.

Did You Know?

○ Approximately 10 percent of all audio recording engineers are self-employed.

○ More audio recording engineers are employed by the television industry than by the radio industry.

○ The highest number of television jobs are found in New York, Los Angeles, Chicago, and Washington, D.C. Positions in radio can be found throughout the country.

work up to more responsible positions and often move to larger studios or production companies. Some may eventually become supervisors or administrators, while others turn to teaching to advance their careers.

Earnings

According to the U.S. Department of Labor, the mean earnings for audio recording technicians employed in the radio and television industries were approximately $31,980 in 2002. Audio recording engineers employed in all industries had earnings that ranged from less than $14,600 to $65,970 or more annually.

Outlook

Employment in this field is expected to grow at an average rate. Computer technology will continue to make the recording process easier, which may limit some jobs for entry-level studio technicians. However, as the television and film industries grow and the recording process becomes faster, more audio recording engineers will be needed. The radio industry has undergone considerable consolidation over the last decade. This has created fewer employment opportunities for audio recording engineers. Engineers with an understanding of advanced technologies, such as digital recording and multimedia, will have an edge over the competition.

FOR MORE INFO

For information on audio recording schools and courses, contact
Audio Engineering Society
60 East 42nd Street, Room 2520
New York, NY 10165-2520
Tel: 212-661-8528
Email: hq@aes.org
http://www.aes.org

For facts and statistics about the recording industry, contact
Recording Industry Association of America
1330 Connecticut Avenue, NW, Suite 300
Washington, DC 20036
Tel: 202-775-0101
http://www.riaa.com

For general information, contact
Society of Professional Audio Recording Services
PO Box 770845
Memphis, TN 38177-0845
Tel: 800-771-7727
Email: spars@spars.com
http://www.spars.com

Broadcast Engineers

What Broadcast Engineers Do

Broadcast engineers, also called *broadcast technicians,* operate the electronic equipment that sends radio and television signals to the public. They are responsible for the operation, installation, and repair of the equipment.

While many broadcast engineers work in the studio, others, called *field technicians,* set up and operate portable radio and television transmitting equipment at locations away from the main station. For example, a radio station may broadcast several hours of programming from a concert venue, or a television station may broadcast a news report live from city hall. Field technicians link microphones, mini-cameras, and amplifiers with the main station by using telephone lines. If the location of the broadcast is too far away for a telephone connection, the broadcast engineer will set up, test, and operate portable microwave transmitters. Sometimes these transmitters beam their signals directly to the main station's receivers; at other times, the engineer will position the transmitter's signals toward an orbiting satellite. The satellite then relays the signal back down to the main stations.

Field technicians usually travel to the site of a broadcast in a specially equipped van. The van carries the

Books to Read

Fountain, Henry. *The New York Times Circuits: How Electronic Things Work.* New York: St. Martin's Press, 2001.

Tozer, EPJ. *Broadcast Engineer's Reference Book.* Burlington, Mass.: Focal Press, 2004.

Warring, R. H. *Building & Designing Transistor Radios: A Beginner's Guide.* Cambridge, U.K.: Lutterworth Press, 2001.

Wilson, David. *A Broadcast Engineering Tutorial for Non-Engineers.* Washington, D.C.: National Association of Broadcasters, 1999.

transmitting equipment, microphones, cameras, lighting equipment, and power sources needed for the broadcast. The van also carries any tools or parts the technicians may need to make minor repairs. Broadcast engineers must be able to use electrical test meters to make sure their equipment is operating properly.

The broadcast engineer monitors the transmitting equipment as the broadcast is being sent back to the main station. Often a broadcast is taped and not played on the air until later.

Chief engineers in both radio and television oversee the entire technical operation and supervise the activities of all the technicians to ensure smooth programming. He or she is also responsible for the budget and must keep abreast of new broadcast communications technology.

Larger stations also have an *assistant chief engineer* who manages the daily activities of the technical crew, controls the maintenance of the electronic equipment, and ensures the performance standards of the station.

Engineers doing maintenance work may have to climb poles and antenna towers, while those on the ground may set up heavy equipment.

Broadcast engineers must have both an aptitude for working with highly technical electronic and computer equipment and minute attention to detail to be successful in the field. They should enjoy both the technical and artistic aspects of working in the radio or television industries. They should also be able to communicate with a wide range of people with various levels of technical expertise.

EXPLORING

○ Read *Broadcast Engineering* (http://www.broadcastengineering.com), a trade publication for broadcast engineers.

○ Participate in school clubs or activities that deal with electronics, cameras, computers, or video equipment.

○ Build and operate an amateur, or ham, radio and experiment with electronic kits.

○ Volunteer at a local radio or television station.

○ Take tours of radio and television studios in your community.

Did You Know?

○ Approximately 32 percent of all broadcast engineers are employed in the radio and television industries.

○ Ten percent of broadcast engineers are self-employed.

○ Since most radio and television stations operate seven days a week, 24-hours a day, broadcast engineers are often required to work on evenings, weekends, and holidays.

Source: U.S. Department of Labor

Education and Training

If you are interested in a career as a broadcast engineer, take courses in mathematics, physics, the physical sciences, and computers in high school.

After high school, you should complete at least a two-year broadcast engineering program at a community college or technical school.

Beginners usually learn from watching experienced technicians while on the job. You may start out at a smaller station, where you will learn important basic skills, and then move on to a larger station, where this experience can help you land a job.

Earnings

Broadcast engineers earned median salaries of $27,760 in 2002, according to the U.S. Department of Labor. The department also reported that the lowest paid 10 percent earned less than $14,600 and the highest paid 10 percent earned more than $65,970 during that same period. Experience, job location, and educational background are all factors that influence a person's pay.

Outlook

Employment for broadcast engineers is expected to grow about as fast as the average for all occupations over the next decade. There will be strong competition for jobs in large cities. Slow growth, industry consolidation, and labor-saving technical advancements in the radio and television industries may mean fewer new job openings in this field. Technicians who are able to install transmitters will have an easier time finding a job as television stations switch from older analog transmitters to new digital transmitters. Job openings will also turn up when existing engineers leave the industry for other jobs in electronics.

Camera Operators

What Camera Operators Do

Camera operators use cameras and related equipment to photograph subjects or material for television programs, commercials, videos, and movies. Camera operators may work on feature films in Hollywood or on location elsewhere. Camera operators who work in television broadcasting studios are often known as *studio camera operators*. They videotape live news broadcasts or other programming, such as talk or variety shows that are prerecorded and broadcast at a later time. *News camera operators* videotape newsworthy events as they happen. They videotape live events—such as press conferences, protests, or natural disasters—and relay this footage to their broadcast affiliate.

The nature of the camera operator's work depends largely on the size of the production crew. When shooting a documentary or short news segment, the camera operator may be responsible for setting up the camera and lighting equipment and for positioning actors or interview subjects during filming. Equipment that camera operators typically use include cranes, dollies, mounting heads, and different types of lenses and accessories. The camera operator is often also responsible for maintenance and repair of all of this equipment.

With a larger crew, the camera operator is responsible only for the

> ## Top Skills for Camera Operators
>
> ○ imagination
> ○ creativity
> ○ knowledge of cameras and related technology
> ○ a "good eye" for the artistic and technical nature of setting up shots
> ○ ability to work well with others
> ○ ability to follow directions

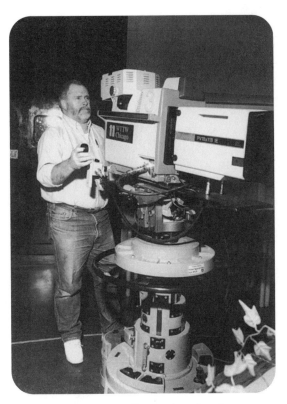

Camera operators usually stand so that they can move the camera quickly from side to side and up and down to catch all the action. (Mathew Hohmann)

actual filming. The camera operator may even have a support team of assistants. The *first assistant camera operator* will typically focus on the cameras, making sure they are loaded and operating correctly. In larger productions, there are also backup cameras and accessories for use if one should malfunction during filming. *Second assistant camera operators* help the first assistant set up scenes to be filmed and assist in the maintenance of the equipment.

Sometimes camera operators must use shoulder-held cameras. This often occurs during the filming of action scenes for television or motion pictures. *Special effects camera operators* photograph the optical effects segments for television and motion pictures. They create visual illusions that can add mood and tone to the production.

Education and Training

In high school, take photography, journalism, and media arts classes. Mathematics and science can help you understand cameras and filters. You should also take art and art history classes and other courses that will help you develop an appreciation of visual styles.

A college degree is not necessary to get a position as a camera operator, but enrolling in film school can help you expand your network of connections. A bachelor's degree in liberal arts or film studies provides a good background for work in the television and film industries. However, practical experience and industry connections will provide the best opportunities for work.

Earnings

Salaries vary widely for camera operators. The U.S. Department of Labor reports that television, video, and movie camera operators earned median annual salaries of $32,720 in 2002. The department also reports that the lowest paid 10 percent of operators earned less than $14,710 per year, and the highest earning 10 percent made more than $65,070 annually. Camera operators employed in television broadcasting earned annual mean salaries of $31,820 in 2002, while those employed in the cable television industry earned $35,890 annually.

EXPLORING

○ Join a photography or camera club or become involved with the media department of your school. You may have the opportunity to videotape sports events, concerts, and school plays.
○ Offer to work part time or volunteer at a camera shop. This will give you a basic understanding of photographic equipment.
○ If your school has a television station, see if you can learn the basics of camera operation.

Read All about It

Learn about the television and film industries by reading these publications:

American Cinematographer
http://www.theasc.com/magazine

Cinefex
http://www.cinefex.com

CineMedia
Web: http://www.cinemedia.org

Daily Variety
http://www.variety.com

Hollywood Reporter
http://www.hollywoodreporter.com

Outlook

Employment for camera operators is expected to increase about as fast as the average for all occupations in the coming years. The use of visual images continues to grow in areas such as communication, education, entertainment, marketing, and research and development. More businesses will make use of video training films and public relations projects that use film. The entertainment industries are also expanding. However, competition for positions will remain very fierce. Camera operators work in what is considered a desirable and exciting field, and they must work hard and be aggressive to get good jobs, especially in Los Angeles and New York.

FOR MORE INFO

For lists of film schools and advice from members, visit the ASC website.
American Society of Cinematographers (ASC)
PO Box 2230
Hollywood, CA 90078
Tel: 800-448-0145
Email: info@theasc.com
http://www.theasc.com

For information on membership benefits, contact this branch of the International Alliance of Theatrical Stage Employees (IATSE).
International Cinematographers Guild (IATSE Local 600)
National Office/Western Region
7715 Sunset Boulevard, Suite 300
Hollywood, CA 90046

Tel: 323-876-0160
http://www.cameraguild.com

To learn about student chapters sponsored by the SMPTE, contact
Society of Motion Picture and Television Engineers (SMPTE)
595 West Hartsdale Avenue
White Plains, NY 10607
Tel: 914-761-1100
Email: smpte@smpte.org
http://www.smpte.org

Visit this website organized by the ASC for a list of film schools and to learn about the career of cinematographer—the next step on the career ladder for camera operators.
Cinematographer.com
http://www.uemedia.com/CPC/cinematographer

Disc Jockeys

What Disc Jockeys Do

Disc jockeys, or *DJs,* play recorded music on the radio or during parties, dances, and special occasions. On the radio they also announce the time, the weather forecast, and important news. Sometimes DJs interview guests, take calls from listeners, and make public service announcements.

Unlike radio and television newscasters, disc jockeys most often do not have to read from a written script, except for scripted commercials. Their comments are usually spontaneous. Most radio shows are broadcast live, and since anything may happen while DJs are on the air, they must react calmly under stress and know how to handle unexpected events. The best disc jockeys have pleasant, soothing voices and a talent for keeping listeners entertained.

Disc jockeys often work irregular hours, and most work alone. Some have to report for work very early in the morning or late at night, because so many radio stations broadcast 24 hours a day. Work in radio stations is demanding. Every activity or comment on the air must begin and end exactly on time. This can be difficult, especially when the disc jockey has to handle news, commercials, music, weather, and guests within

The First Celebrity DJ

The first major contemporary disc jockey in the United States was Alan Freed (1921–65). Freed worked in the 1950s on WINS radio in New York. In 1957, his rock and roll stage shows at the Paramount Theater made front-page news in the *New York Times* because of the huge crowds they attracted.

EXPLORING

○ Participate in debate or speech clubs to work on your speaking skills and your ability to think and react quickly.

○ Try to get a summer job at a radio station.

○ Take advantage of any opportunity to speak or perform before an audience. Try any type of announcing, such as at sports events, awards dinners, or school dances.

○ Offer to be the DJ at friends' parties or school dances.

○ Record yourself introducing your favorite songs, reading a short news report, or giving weather or traffic information.

a certain time frame. It takes a lot of skill to work the controls, watch the clock, select music, talk with guests or listeners, read reports, and entertain the audience. Usually several of these tasks must be performed at the same time.

Disc jockeys must always be aware of pleasing their audiences. They play the music their listeners like and talk about the things their listeners want to talk about. If listeners begin to switch stations, ratings go down, and disc jockeys can lose their jobs. DJs who become popular with their audiences and stay with a station for a long time sometimes become famous local personalities.

Education and Training

In high school, take English classes and speech classes to help you develop your communication abilities. Extracurricular activities such as debating and theater will also help you learn good pronunciation and projection. Music classes will introduce you to musical styles, techniques, and artists. If your high school has a radio station, be sure to volunteer as a disc jockey, producer, or technician.

There is no formal education required for disc jockeys. Many large radio stations prefer to hire people who have had some college education. Some schools train students for broadcasting, but such training will not necessarily improve the chances of finding a job at a radio station. When hiring DJs, station managers consider an applicant's personality and listen carefully to audition tapes.

If you want to become a disc jockey and possibly advance to other broadcasting positions, attend a college or technical school that has broadcasting or announcing programs. Working at a college radio station can give you valuable experience. Many DJs start out at small radio stations operating equipment and taping interviews.

Earnings

Disc jockeys earned anywhere from $12,770 to more than $51,830 annually in 2002, according to the U.S. Department of Labor. The average salary was $20,620 a year. Those who work for small stations earn the lowest salaries. Top personalities in large

A disc jockey announces the next recording to be played on his radio show. (Mathew Hohmann)

Did You Know?

○ The average American listens to radio three hours during the week and five hours on weekends, according to the National Association of Broadcasters.

○ There were 13,383 radio stations in the United States in March 2003, according to the Federal Communications Commission.

○ There were more than 44,000 radio stations in the world in 2000, according to the *CIA World Factbook*.

○ The top three radio formats, according to Arbitron, are news/talk/information, adult contemporary, and contemporary hit radio.

market stations earn salaries that range from $100,000 to more than $1 million annually.

Outlook

In the broadcasting field there are usually more job applicants than job openings. As a result, competition is stiff. Beginning jobs in small radio stations usually are easiest to find. Employment of disc jockeys is expected to decline over the next several years. Due to this decline, competition will be great in an already competitive field.

Small stations will still hire beginners, but on-air experience will be increasingly important. You may have an advantage over other job applicants if you know a lot about a specific area such as business, political, or health news, or if you have an extensive knowledge of a particular kind of music, such as jazz, rock, or country.

Lighting Technicians

What Lighting Technicians Do

Lighting technicians set up and control the lighting equipment for television and movie productions. These technicians are sometimes known as *assistant chief set electricians* or *lights operators*. A lighting technician who is responsible for the lighting of an entire television show or film is called the *chief lighting technician* or *gaffer.*

When a television show is being planned, lighting technicians talk with the director of the show to find out what types of lighting and special lighting effects will be used. Lighting technicians then arrange the equipment they will need to produce the required lighting effects. For example, if the script calls for sunshine to be streaming in through a window, technicians set up lights to produce this effect. Other effects they may be asked to produce include lighting the flash from an explosion or the soft glow of a room lit with old-fashioned oil lamps.

If the television program is a weekly series that is always filmed or taped on the same set, the lights will already be in position. Otherwise, the lights will have to be set up. If the production is small, the technicians will set up the lights themselves. At large television stations, assistants set up the lights following the chief lighting technician's instructions.

During the broadcast, lighting technicians work in a control room and follow a special script. The script

Learn More about It

Visit this site to explore different theater jobs and play an interactive game about lighting a scene.

Kids Work!

http://www.knowitall.org/kidswork/theater/
jobplay/ltdesigner

EXPLORING

○ Watch television shows and movies to see different lighting effects.

○ Work the lighting for a school stage production.

○ Join your school's newspaper or yearbook staff and practice working with cameras. Experiment with different lighting options.

○ Ask if you can film a school play, concert, or sporting event. Before the event, figure out what lighting will be used and how to best film it.

tells them which lighting effects are needed at what times during the broadcast. As the show is taped, the lighting technicians watch the broadcast on television monitors in the control room. This allows them to see their work and to make any necessary adjustments.

The movie industry also employs lighting technicians. These technicians usually work with much larger groups of lights, and the conditions under which they work—outdoors or at night—are especially challenging. Live concerts also require lighting technicians. Live theater productions employ lighting technicians, who are responsible for creating realistic and magical lighting effects on stage.

Setting up lights can be demanding work, especially when lighting a large movie set. Technicians should be able to handle heavy lights on stands and work with suspended lights while on a ladder. They should be able to work with electricians' hand tools (screwdrivers, pliers, and so forth) and be comfortable working with electricity. Lighting technicians should also be dependable and capable of working as part of a team.

Education and Training

In high school, you should learn as much as possible about electronics, television production, and working with cameras. Courses in physics and math are also important. Good communication skills are essential for working with the various people on the television or movie set.

After high school, seek out community colleges and technical schools that offer programs in electronics and broadcast technology. If you would like to advance to a technical management position, you should consider earning a college degree in electrical or electronics engineering.

Lighting technicians discuss the arrangement of lights for an upcoming production. (NYS Theatre Institute)

Earnings

Salaries for lighting technicians vary according to the technician's experience. Annual income is also determined by the number of projects a technician handles a year. The most experienced technicians can work year-round on a variety of projects, while those starting out may go weeks without work. According to the International Alliance of Theatrical Stage Employees, Moving Picture Technicians, Artists and Allied Crafts, the union that represents lighting technicians, the minimum hourly pay for unionized gaffers was $22.50 in 2000. Other lighting technicians earned at least $16.50 to $20.50 an hour. Experienced technicians can negotiate for much higher wages.

Lights

Need a baby-baby? A midget? A nooklite? An inbetweenie?

Visit http://www.mole.com, the website for the Mole-Richardson Co., to read about lighting equipment used in Hollywood. At the site, you will see pictures of a variety of different kinds of lighting products in its online catalog, and get a sense of some of the lingo of the profession.

FOR MORE INFO

Visit this site for interviews with award-winning cinematographers, a "tricks of the trade" page, information about film schools, multimedia presentations, and the American Cinematographer *online magazine.*

American Society of Cinematographers
PO Box 2230
Hollywood, CA 90078
Tel: 800-448-0145
http://www.theasc.com

For information on union membership, contact

International Alliance of Theatrical Stage Employees, Moving Picture Technicians, Artists and Allied Crafts
1430 Broadway, 20th Floor
New York, NY 10018
Tel: 212-730-1770
http://www.iatse-intl.org

Outlook

As long as the television and movie industries continue to grow, there will be job opportunities for lighting technicians. With the expansion of the cable television market, lighting technicians may find work in more than one area. Persistence and hard work are required in order to secure a good job in television or film.

The increasing use of visual effects and computer-generated imagery will likely have an impact on the work of lighting technicians. Through computer programs, filmmakers and editors can adjust lighting themselves. However, live-action shots are still integral to the filmmaking process and will remain so for some time. Getting the initial shots of a television show or film requires sophisticated lighting equipment and trained technicians. Lighting technicians often have to know about the assembly and operation of more pieces of equipment than anyone else working on a production. In the future, equipment will become more compact and mobile, making the technician's job easier.

Media Planners and Buyers

What Media Planners and Buyers Do

Media specialists place advertisements that will reach specific customers. Media specialists try to get the best response from the market for the least amount of money. *Media planners* gather information about the sizes and types of audiences that can be reached through various media (radio, TV, print, Web) and about the cost of advertising in each medium. *Media buyers* purchase space in printed publications, on billboards and the Internet, and on radio or television stations. Advertising media workers are supervised by a *media director.* The media director is accountable for the overall media plan. In addition to advertising agencies, media planners and buyers work for large companies, such as film studios, television networks, and radio stations, that purchase space or broadcast time. These media specialists must be familiar with the markets that each medium reaches, as well as the advantages and disadvantages of advertising in each.

Media planners determine target markets based on their clients' advertising needs. For example, if a television studio wanted to advertise its new family comedy, media planners would gather information about the public's viewing,

Personal and Professional Skills

- strong understanding of television, film, or radio industries
- knowledge of consumer buying trends
- problem-solving abilities
- creativity
- excellent oral, written, and analytical skills
- ability to handle multiple assignments

reading, and buying habits by administering questionnaires and conducting other forms of market research. Through this research, planners would identify target markets (in this case, parents, children, and so forth). By knowing which people watch certain TV shows, listen to specific radio stations, or read particular magazines or newspapers, media planners can help the television network select air time or print space to reach the consumers most likely to watch the movie. For example, Saturday morning cartoons attract children, while prime-time programs often draw family audiences. These would be excellent places to advertise the new comedy show since these groups make up a large segment of potential viewers. Media planners might also choose to advertise the new show in a special kid's section of the newspaper or on a weekly radio show that is popular with families.

Media buyers do the actual purchasing of the time on radio or television or the space in a newspaper or magazine in which an advertisement will run. In addition to tracking the time and space available for purchase, media buyers ensure that ads appear when and where they should, negotiate costs for ad placement, and calculate rates, usage, and budgets. They are also responsible for maintaining contact with clients, keeping them informed of all advertising-related developments, and resolving any conflicts that arise.

Workers who actually sell the print space or air time to advertisers are called *print sales workers* or *broadcast time salespeople*. Like media planners, these professionals are well versed about the target markets served by their organizations and can often provide useful information about editorial content or broadcast programs.

EXPLORING

○ Work as a production assistant, programmer, writer, or editor in your school's media department.

○ Work as an advertising salesperson for your school's yearbook or theatre department.

○ Volunteer or work part time for the classified advertising department of your local newspaper.

○ Choose a popular television or radio show and determine its target audience and the best advertising methods to reach this group of people.

Words to Learn

advertisement paid announcement of a product or service to the public

advertising agency group of researchers, writers, artists, buyers of space and time, other specialists, and account executives who design and execute advertising programs for clients

electronic banners the Internet equivalent of billboard advertising, which accounts for 80 percent of online ads

market research study of consumer groups to determine personal interests and characteristics

media avenues through which advertisers can place ads, including the Internet, television, radio, magazines, newspapers, and outdoor signs

target audience group of consumers that is considered the most likely to purchase a product; also known as **target market**

time slot specific time that a commercial will air on radio or television

Interactive media specialists are responsible for managing all critical aspects of their clients' online advertising campaigns. While interactive media planners may have responsibilities similar to those of print or broadcast planners, they also act as new technology specialists, placing and tracking all online ads and maintaining relationships with clients and webmasters alike.

Education and Training

You can prepare for a future job as media planner and/or buyer by taking specific courses in high school. These include business, marketing, economics, advertising, radio and television, and film and video. General liberal arts classes, such as English, communications, and journalism, are also important, since media planners and buyers must be able to communicate clearly with both clients and coworkers. In addition, mathematics classes will give you the skills to work accurately with budgets and placement costs.

Increasingly, media planners and buyers have college degrees, often with majors in marketing or advertising. Even if you have prior work experience or training in media, you

FOR MORE INFO

For information on the advertising industry, contact

American Advertising Federation (AAF)
1101 Vermont Avenue, NW, Suite 500
Washington, DC 20005-6306
Email: aaf@aaf.org
http://www.aaf.org

should select college classes that provide a good balance of business coursework, broadcast and print experience, and liberal arts studies.

Earnings

Because media planners and buyers work for a variety of organizations across the country and abroad, earnings can vary greatly. Advertising sales agents had median annual earnings of $37,670 in 2002, according to the U.S. Department of Labor. Salaries ranged from less than $19,430 to more than $87,560. Media directors can earn between $46,000 and $120,000 depending on the type of employer and the director's experience level.

Some salespeople draw straight salaries, some receive bonuses that reflect their level of sales, and still others earn their entire wage based on commissions. These commissions are usually calculated as a percentage of sales that the employee brings into the company.

Outlook

The employment outlook for media planners and buyers, like the outlook for the advertising industry itself, depends on the general health of the economy. When the economy thrives, companies produce an increasing number of goods and seek to promote them via newspapers, magazines, television, radio, the Internet, and various other media. The U.S. Department of Labor anticipates that employment in the advertising industry is projected to grow faster than the average for all occupations.

Competition for all advertising positions, including entry-level jobs, is expected to be intense. Media planners and buyers who have considerable experience will have the best chances of finding employment.

Radio and Television Anchors

What Radio and Television Anchors Do

The announcer who specializes in reporting the news to the listening or viewing public is called an *anchor* or *newscaster*. This job may require simply reporting facts, or it may include editorial commentary. Sometimes anchors have the authority to express their opinions on news items or the philosophies of others. They must make judgments about which news is important and which is not. In some instances, they write their own scripts, based on facts that are furnished by international news bureaus and other sources. In other instances, they read text exactly as it appears on a teletype machine or TelePrompTer. They may make as few as one or two reports each day if they work on a major news program, or they may broadcast news for five minutes every hour or half-hour. Their delivery is usually dignified, measured, and impersonal.

Many television and radio anchors have become well-known public personalities in broadcasting. They may

Words to Learn

audition tape sent by applicants to stations where they would like to work

FCC Federal Communications Commission; an independent federal agency that regulates television, cable, and radio

newscast news program that airs the news on television or radio

ratings determined by Nielsen (television) or Arbitron (radio), ratings help rank the stations and attract advertising dollars

script written copy read by anchors and reporters

TelePrompTer for television broadcasts, this machine projects the script for on-air anchors to read

EXPLORING

- Try to get a summer job at a radio or television station.
- Ask your teacher to set up an informational interview with a news anchor.
- Tour a radio or television news station.
- Take any opportunity to speak or perform before an audience.
- Join the speech or debate team to build your communication skills.
- Work on your school's newspaper or television or radio station.

participate in community activities as masters of ceremonies at banquets and other public events and write articles and books about news-related issues.

Education and Training

In high school, take a college preparatory curriculum that will teach you how to write and use the English language in literature and communication classes, including speech. Subjects such as history, government, economics, and a foreign language are also important.

Although there are no formal educational requirements for becoming a radio or television anchor, most large stations will only consider college-educated applicants. Announcers with broad educational and cultural backgrounds are better prepared to successfully meet a variety of unexpected or emergency situations. The more knowledge of geography, history, literature, the arts, political science, music, science, and of the sound and structure of the English language that an anchor has, the greater his or her value.

Aspiring news anchors typically receive college degrees in journalism, English, political science, economics, telecommunications, or communications.

Earnings

Television news anchors earn higher salaries than anchors who are employed in radio. Television anchors earned average salaries of $69,800 in 2001, according to a salary survey by the Radio-Television News Directors Association. Salaries ranged from $17,000 to more than $1 million annually. For radio news anchors, the average salary was $30,500 in 2001 with a low of $10,000 and a high of $150,000.

For both radio and television, salaries are higher in the larger markets. Salaries are also generally higher in commercial than in public broadcasting. Nationally known anchors and newscasters—such as Tom Brokaw, Peter Jennings, and Dan Rather—who appear regularly on network television programs receive salaries in the millions.

Read about Famous Anchors on the Web

David Brinkley
http://www.museum.tv/archives/etv/B/htmlB/brinkleydav/brinkleydav.htm

Tom Brokaw
http://www.msnbc.com/onair/bios/t_brokaw.asp

Walter Cronkite
http://www.museum.tv/archives/etv/C/htmlC/cronkitewal/cronkitewal.htm

Lester Holt
http://www.msnbc.com/news/453174.asp

Peter Jennings
http://abcnews.go.com/sections/wnt/WorldNewsTonight/jennings_peter_bio.html

Dan Rather
http://www.cbsnews.com/stories/2002/02/25/eveningnews/main502026.shtml

Carole Simpson
http://abcnews.go.com/sections/wnt/WorldNewsSaturday/simpson_carole_bio.html

Paula Zahn
http://www.cnn.com/CNN/anchors_reporters/zahn.paula.html

Outlook

Competition for entry-level employment in this career during the coming years is expected to be keen, as the broadcasting industry always attracts more applicants than there are jobs. Applicants will have a better chance of working in radio than in television because there are more radio stations. Local television stations usually carry a high percentage of network programs and need only a small staff to carry out local operations.

The U.S. Department of Labor predicts that opportunities for anchors will grow more slowly than the average over the next several years due to the slowing growth of new radio and television stations. Openings will result mainly from those who leave the industry or the labor force.

FOR MORE INFO

For information about broadcast education and the broadcasting industry, contact
Broadcast Education Association
1771 N Street, NW
Washington, DC 20036-2891
Tel: 202-429-5354
Email: beainfo@beaweb.org
http://www.beaweb.org

To read answers to frequently asked questions about broadcasting, visit the NAB website.
National Association of Broadcasters (NAB)
1771 N Street, NW
Washington, DC 20036-2891
Tel: 202-429-5300
Email: nab@nab.org
http://www.nab.org

For information on the cable television industry, contact
National Cable and Telecommunications Association
1724 Massachusetts Avenue, NW
Washington, DC 20036
Tel: 202-775-3550
http://www.ncta.com

For industry information, contact
Radio-Television News Directors Association
1600 K Street, NW, Suite 700
Washington, DC 20006-2838
Tel: 202-659-6510
Email: rtnda@rtnda.org
http://www.rtnda.org

Radio and Television Program Directors

What Radio and Television Program Directors Do

Radio and television program directors plan and schedule programs for radio and television stations and networks. They work in both commercial and public broadcasting and work for individual radio or television stations, regional or national networks, or cable television systems.

Program directors work on entertainment and public service programs, newscasts, sportscasts, and commercial announcements. Program directors decide what material is broadcast and when it is scheduled. They work with other staff members to develop programs and buy programs from independent producers. They are guided by such factors as the budget available for program material, the intended audience, station and federal policy on content, and the products advertised in commercials. Program directors must understand their listeners, viewers, advertisers, and sponsors and be able to adapt programming to meet their needs.

Top Five Radio Markets

1. New York, N.Y.
2. Los Angeles, Calif.
3. Chicago, Ill.
4. San Francisco, Calif.
5. Dallas-Ft. Worth, Texas

Top Five Television Markets

1. New York, N.Y.
2. Los Angeles, Calif.
3. Chicago, Ill.
4. Philadelphia, Pa.
5. San Francisco-Oakland-San Jose, Calif.

Source: Nielsen Media Research

To Be a Successful Program Director, You Should . . .

○ be creative
○ be adaptable
○ have the ability to work under deadline pressure
○ be willing to work long hours when necessary
○ have the ability to work with all types of people—from on-air talent to sales workers to clerical staff
○ possess strong management and organizational skills

Program directors also set schedules for the program staff, audition and hire announcers and anchors, and assist the sales department in negotiating contracts with commercial sponsors. Program directors' duties vary depending on whether they work in radio or television, the size of their station or a network, or whether they work for a commercial or public operation.

Some larger stations and networks employ *public service directors,* who plan and schedule radio or television public service programs and announcements. These may be in such fields as education, religion, and civic and government affairs. *Broadcast operations directors* coordinate the activities of the personnel who prepare network program schedules, review program schedules, issue daily corrections, and advise affiliated stations on their schedules. Other managers in radio and television broadcasting include production managers, operations directors, music directors, news directors, and sports directors.

Education and Training

English, debate, and speech classes are good preparation for this career. Business courses are also helpful.

A college degree is recommended for this field. Possible majors for those interested in this work include radio and television production and broadcasting, communications, liberal arts, or business administration. Technical training will help you understand the engineering aspects of broadcasting. Experience at a radio or television station is important. Many program directors move into their positions after working for a number of years as a music director, as a staff announcer, or in some other capacity at a station.

Earnings

Salaries for radio and television program directors vary widely based on such factors as size and location of the station, whether the station is commercial or public, and experience of the director. Television program directors generally earn more than program directors in radio. According to the U.S. Bureau of Labor Statistics, median annual earnings of general and operations managers in radio and television broadcasting were $79,019 in 2002.

According to a salary survey by the Radio and Television News Directors Association, radio news directors earned a median annual salary of $30,500 in 2001. Salaries ranged from a low of $10,000 to a high of $72,000. Television news directors earned a median salary of $64,000, with earnings ranging from $18,000 to $250,000.

Both radio and television program directors usually receive health and life coverage benefits and sometimes yearly bonuses as well.

Outlook

Employment growth in radio and television broadcasting is expected to be slower than the average in the next decade. The slow growth rate is attributed to industry consolidation,

EXPLORING

○ Volunteer to help at small radio stations or local cable stations.
○ Take tours of radio and television stations in your area.
○ Volunteer to work on school committees in charge of planning and directing special events.

introduction of new technologies, greater use of prepared programming, and competition from other media.

Competition for radio and television program director jobs is strong. There are more opportunities for beginners in radio than there are in television. Most radio and television stations in large cities hire only experienced workers. New radio and television stations and new cable television systems are expected to create some openings for program directors. Some radio stations are eliminating program director positions by installing automatic programming equipment or combining those responsibilities with other positions.

FOR MORE INFO

For information about broadcast education and the broadcasting industry, contact
Broadcast Education Association
1771 N Street, NW
Washington, DC 20036-2891
Tel: 202-429-5354
Email: beainfo@beaweb.org
http://www.beaweb.org

To read answers to frequently asked questions about broadcasting, visit the NAB website.
National Association of Broadcasters (NAB)
1771 N Street, NW
Washington, DC 20036-2891
Tel: 202-429-5300
Email: nab@nab.org
http://www.nab.org

For information on the cable television industry, contact

National Cable and Telecommunications Association
1724 Massachusetts Avenue, NW
Washington, DC 20036
Tel: 202-775-3550
http://www.ncta.com

For industry information, contact
Radio and Television News Directors Association
1600 K Street, NW, Suite 700
Washington, DC 20006-2838
Tel: 202-659-6510
Email: rtnda@rtnda.org
http://www.rtnda.org

For career information and an overview of the industry, visit
About.com: Radio
http://radio.about.com

Radio Producers

What Radio Producers Do

Radio producers plan, rehearse, and produce live or recorded programs. They work with on-air personnel; behind-the-scenes with workers, music, sound effects; and with technology to put together a radio show. In many situations, particularly with smaller radio stations, the disc jockey and the show's producer are the same person.

Radio producers study the marketplace by listening to other area radio stations and determining what's needed and appreciated in the community. They conduct surveys and interviews to find out what the public wants to hear. They decide which age groups they want to pursue and develop a format based on what appeals to these listeners. This all results in establishing a station's identity, which is very important. Listeners associate a station with the kind of music it plays, how much music it plays, the type of news and conversation presented, and the station's on-air personalities.

Based on listener feedback and on market research, radio *disc jockeys, program directors,* and producers determine what music to play and create music libraries that will help the station develop a unique on-air identity. Producers also keep track of current events. They consult newspapers and radio programs to determine what subjects to discuss on their shows.

Did You Know?

- Radio reaches 94 percent of all consumers each week.
- Americans listen to 20 hours of radio on average a week.
- As of March 2003, there were 4,804 AM stations and 8,579 FM stations in the United States.

EXPLORING

○ Listen to all types of radio shows as often as possible. What are your favorite shows and why? How would you improve radio shows or stations that you do not like?

○ Volunteer your services to a small radio station in your area.

○ Some high schools have on-site radio stations that allow you to get hands-on experience.

○ Get involved in management and planning for school and community clubs.

Producers have to keep a show running on time, which involves carefully weaving many elements into a show, including music, news reports, interviews, and commercials. They write copy for and coordinate on-air commercials, which are usually recorded in advance. They also devise contests, from large public events to small, on-air trivia competitions.

Though a majority of radio stations have music formats, radio producers also work for 24-hour news, public broadcasting, and talk radio stations. Producing news programs and radio documentaries involves a great deal of research and skill in booking guests, writing scripts, and interviewing.

Education and Training

Writing skills are especially valuable if you want to work in radio. In high school, take English and social science courses that require essays and term papers. Journalism classes will not only help you develop your writing skills but also teach you about the nature and history of media.

After high school, look for a college with schools of journalism or communications that offer programs in broadcasting. Business courses will help you prepare for a career as a producer. Radio producers often start their training in journalism schools and receive hands-on instruction at campus radio stations. Radio station news directors and program directors generally want to hire people who have a well-rounded education with knowledge of history, geography, political science, and literature.

Earnings

According to the U.S. Department of Labor radio producers earned mean annual salaries of $47,490 in 2002. Salaries ranged from $23,000 or less to more than $119,000 annually. Like many radio jobs, there is a wide salary range resulting from differences in market size and the size of each radio station. Most large stations offer full-time employees typical benefits, including health and life insurance.

Outlook

Employment growth in the radio industry is expected to be slower than the average over the next decade. Today, radio stations are bought and sold at a rapid pace. Mergers often result in radio stations having to change formats as well as entire staffs. Though some radio producers are able to stay at a station over a period of several years, people going into radio should

Words to Learn

AM broadcast   amplitude modulation system of radio broadcasting

Arbitron ratings   ratings provided within local markets to identify how many people are listening to different radio stations; these ratings also identify listeners by age, gender, buying patterns, and other demographic information

FM broadcast   frequency modulation method of radio broadcasting

market   geographic area served by a radio station

playlist   list of recordings that will be played during a radio program or time period

ratings   estimate of radio listeners during a specific time period

FOR MORE INFO

For information about broadcast education and the broadcasting industry, contact
Broadcast Education Association
1771 N Street, NW
Washington, DC 20036-2891
Tel: 202-429-5354
Email: beainfo@beaweb.org
http://www.beaweb.org

To read answers to frequently asked questions about broadcasting, visit the NAB website.
National Association of Broadcasters (NAB)
1771 N Street, NW
Washington, DC 20036-2891
Tel: 202-429-5300
Email: nab@nab.org
http://www.nab.org

For career information and an overview of the industry, visit
About.com: Radio
http://radio.about.com

be prepared to change employers at some point in their careers.

Another trend that is affecting radio producers is the increasing use of programming created by services outside the broadcasting industry. Satellite radio, in which subscribers pay a monthly fee for access to more than 100 radio stations, will be a big threat to smaller, marginal stations.

Competition is stiff for all radio jobs. Graduates of college broadcasting programs are finding a scarcity of work in media. Paid internships will also be difficult to find; many students of radio will have to work for free for a while to gain experience.

Real-Time Captioners

What Real-Time Captioners Do

Real-time captioners, often called *real-time reporters* or *steno-captioners,* create closed captions for live television broadcasts. ("Closed" simply means that the captions may not be seen without special equipment.) Real-time captioners operate a computer-aided transcription stenotype system. This is a modified stenotype machine connected to a computer. This computer translates stenographic keystrokes into words.

Captioners type into the steno machine while listening to a live broadcast, transcribing the broadcast accurately while inserting correct punctuation and other symbols. The computer translates the steno strokes into words that are sent electronically to the broadcast site. Within two to three seconds, people across the country can receive the captions on their television screens.

Captioners produce captions for live television programs, such as local and network news broadcasts, talk shows, and sporting events, for the benefit of citizens who are deaf or hard of hearing. The market for captions has expanded, however, to include other groups, such as people learning English as a second language and those learning to read, especially students with reading disabilities. Captioners work not only in television, but in courtrooms, lawyers' offices, and classrooms.

Who Benefits from Closed-Captioned Programming?

○ deaf and hard of hearing people
○ children and adults learning to read
○ adults learning English as a second language
○ children and adults with learning disabilities

Source: National Captioning Institute Foundation

EXPLORING

○ Practice your transcribing skills by typing taped lectures or television shows.

○ Build your vocabulary skills by reading books and other publications.

○ Increase your awareness of current events, both national and international, by reading newspapers and books and watching television news shows.

○ Ask your teacher to set up an information interview with a real-time captioner.

It takes about one and a half to two hours for a real-time captioner to prepare for an average news broadcast, using preparation materials obtained from the broadcaster and the captioner's own research. Captioners call this pre-show preparation *dictionary-building*. Real-time captioners go through resource materials to find words that might come up during a broadcast, then they develop steno codes that they will use to write these words when they come up during the broadcast.

Real-time captioners are extremely proficient in machine shorthand skills and have strong English grammar, spelling, and comprehension skills. Vocabulary skills also are critical to producing accurate captions, particularly at the required speeds of 200 to 250 words per minute.

Education and Training

Typing and computer courses will increase your keyboard speed and accuracy and help you understand word processing programs. Because you'll be working with a variety of news, sports, and entertainment programs, you should keep up on current events by taking journalism and government courses.

After high school, you should complete the training to become a court and conference reporter (stenographer), which takes from two to four years. An associate's or bachelor's degree in court and conference reporting, or satisfactory completion of other two-year equivalent programs, is usually required. After graduating from court reporting school, captioners undergo three to six months of on-the-job training.

Earnings

Earnings for real-time captioners depend on many variables, especially the geographic region and size of company in which the captioner works. In large captioning organizations, real-time captioners can make anywhere from $28,000 at the entry level to $65,000 or more for very experienced captioners. Trainee salaries increase once the captioner goes on the air.

A real-time captioner creates closed captioning for a professional basketball game. (National Captioning Institute Inc.)

Salaries for real-time captioners are often in line with salaries for court reporters. According to the U.S. Department of Labor, average annual earnings for court reporters were $41,550 in 2002.

A fringe benefit of working for a captioning agency for most reporters (particularly students just out of school) is that such agencies generally provide all the equipment, which costs approximately $15,000. Large captioning organizations also offer benefits, such as paid vacation and health insurance. These benefits are likely to be provided at a courthouse for

Captioning Facts

○ Real-time captioning was introduced by the National Captioning Institute (NCI) in April 1982. The first captioned television show was the Academy Awards.

○ According to the NCI Foundation, more than 100 million people in the United States benefit from captioned programming.

○ The Telecommunications Act of 1996 requires that 95 percent of all new programming on television be captioned by 2006.

FOR MORE INFO

The NCI website features a captioning time line and glossary.
National Captioning Institute (NCI)
1900 Gallows Road, Suite 3000
Vienna, VA 22182
Tel: 703-917-7600
http://www.ncicap.org

Visit the NCRA website for information on captioning careers, tips on developing captioning skills, useful articles, and to participate in an online forum.
National Court Reporters Association (NCRA)
8224 Old Courthouse Road
Vienna, VA 22182-3808
Tel: 800-272-6272
http://www.ncraonline.org

court reporters but not at a freelance firm of deposition reporters, for instance.

Outlook

The National Court Reporters Association reports a decline in enrollment in court reporting schools. This may be because of the development of voice and speech computer systems that automatically convert speech to written text. However, there are no current systems that can accurately handle multiple speakers, and it is unlikely that such technology will be developed in the near future. Therefore, captioners and court reporters will be in high demand for years to come. Digital TV (DTV) will also make captioning more desirable and useful to more people, thereby increasing demand for captioners. DTV enhancements will allow viewers with poor vision to adjust text-size, styles, and fonts. DTV will also allow for more non-English letters, as well as more information transmitted per minute.

With basic real-time skills, captioners will be able to find work in computer-integrated courtrooms; taking real-time depositions for attorneys; providing accompanying litigation support, such as key word indexing; real-timing or captioning in the classroom; or doing broadcast captioning. Other opportunities for the real-time captioner include working with hospitals that specialize in cochlear implants.

Reporters

What Reporters Do

Reporters gather information and report the news for radio, television, magazines, and newspapers. They cover stories on local, national, or international events. *Correspondents* cover stories from a specific area. For example, each national network station has a White House correspondent, a Congressional correspondent, and a Pentagon correspondent.

Reporters and correspondents gather all the information they need to write or broadcast clear and accurate news stories. They interview people, research the facts and history behind a story, observe important events, and then write the story. News stories may be a one-day item, such as a power failure or weather-related piece. Or they may cover a period of days or weeks, on subjects such as trials, investigations, major disasters, and election campaigns.

To gather information, reporters take notes and record or videotape interviews with news sources. Reporters may also examine documents related to the story. Before reporters start putting together their stories, they discuss the importance of

The All-Important Interview

Good reporters are usually good interviewers. They interview experts to get the details of a story. For example, they might talk to an oncologist about a new cancer treatment. Reporters interview eyewitnesses, such as customers who saw a bank robbery or people who lived through a tornado. They interview people to get their opinions on news events, such as citizens who might be affected by the construction of a highway through their neighborhood. Interviews are important for getting the facts, supporting the facts, and getting various sides of the story.

Watch and listen to news reports. How many stories use interviews? What questions did the reporters ask? Did the interviews supply important information? Would the story have been as good without the interviews?

A reporter interviews an elected official after a press conference. (Gibson Stock Photography)

the subject matter with an editor or a producer. *Editors* and *producers* decide what news will be covered each day. They determine how long a story should be and how much importance to give it. Sometimes they decide to hold the story for a while or not to run it at all.

Reporters then organize the information and write a concise, informative story. Reporters and correspondents who are too far from their editorial office to return to file their reports may phone, email, or fax them in.

Because of continual deadline pressure, a reporter's life is hectic. Stories for nightly news broadcasts have to be in and reviewed by the producer before air time. Newspaper articles must be filed long before the first edition is printed, which is usually in the very early hours of the morning. If a major news story takes place, reporters may have to work 18 or 20 hours without a break.

Some correspondents are assigned to cover dangerous areas. War stories are frequently filed from the country where the war is taking place. Reporters who cover riots, floods, major disasters, and other stories must be able to work in difficult, dangerous, and upsetting situations.

Education and Training

You can begin to prepare for a career as a reporter in high school. Take courses in English, writing, history, typing, and computer science. After high school, you should go to college and earn a bachelor's degree in journalism or liberal arts. Master's degrees are becoming more important for journalists, particularly for reporters who specialize in subjects such as science or computer technology.

Earnings

Radio and television reporters had mean annual earnings of $46,260 in 2002, according to the U.S. Department of Labor. Salaries for all reporters ranged from less than

EXPLORING

- ○ Work on a school newspaper or community newsletter. You can offer to be a reporter or writer, or you can help with word processing and printing.
- ○ Watch or listen to newscasts. Follow the work of one or two reporters who cover a topic that interests you, such as sports, politics, science, or culture.
- ○ Talk to reporters at local radio and TV stations. Ask the following questions: What do you like and dislike about your job? What is a typical day like? What skills do reporters need to be successful?

Another Career Option for Reporters

In addition to working on radio or television, many reporters find rewarding careers in the newspaper industry. Visit the following website to access *The Journalist's Road to Success: A Career Guide,* which contains information on careers in print journalism and lists of journalism schools in the United States.

Dow Jones Newspaper Fund
http://djnewspaperfund.dowjones.com/fund/pubcareerguide.asp

FOR MORE INFO

For general educational information on all areas of journalism, including radio and television, contact
Association for Education in Journalism and Mass Communication
234 Outlet Pointe Boulevard
Columbia, SC 29210-5667
Tel: 803-798-0271
Email: aejmchq@aejmc.org
http://www.aejmc.org

For information about broadcast education and the broadcasting industry, contact
Broadcast Education Association
1771 N Street, NW
Washington, DC 20036-2891
Tel: 202-429-5354
Email: beainfo@beaweb.org
http://www.beaweb.org

To read answers to frequently asked questions about broadcasting, visit the NAB website.
National Association of Broadcasters (NAB)
1771 N Street, NW
Washington, DC 20036-2891
Tel: 202-429-5300
Email: nab@nab.org
http://www.nab.org

$17,620 to more than $69,450 in 2002. Television reporters, on average, earn higher salaries than radio reporters. Top national reporters employed by major television networks can earn more than $100,000 annually.

Outlook

Employment for reporters and correspondents is expected to grow more slowly than the average over the next decade. In television and radio news, cutbacks have affected most large stations and all of the networks. Those who major in news-editorial journalism and complete an internship while in school will have the best employment prospects. Competition for reporting jobs at large stations in major markets will be very intense. Most reporters break into the business by applying at stations in small towns or rural areas and gradually work their way up to larger markets as they gain experience and skill.

Screenwriters

What Screenwriters Do

Screenwriters write scripts for television or motion pictures. The themes may be their own ideas or stories assigned by a producer or director. Often, screenwriters are hired to turn popular plays or novels into screenplays. Writers of original screenplays create their own stories, which are produced for the television or film industries. Screenwriters may also write television programs, such as comedies, dramas, documentaries, variety shows, and entertainment specials.

Screenwriters must not only be creative, but they must also have excellent research skills. For projects such as historical movies, documentaries, and medical or science programs, research is a very important step.

Screenwriters start with an outline, or a treatment, of the story's plot. When the director or producer approves the story outline, screenwriters then complete the story for production. During the writing process, screenwriters write many drafts of the script. They frequently meet with directors and producers to discuss script changes.

Some screenwriters work alone and others work with a team of writers. Many specialize in certain types of scripts, such as drama, comedy,

On the Web

Visit this site for articles on screenwriting, interviews with famous screenwriters, and information on free online workshops and resources.

Screenwriters Utopia

http://www.screenwritersutopia.com

For an overview of screenwriting and useful exercises, visit the following website.

Screenwriting: The Language of Film

http://www.oscars.org/teachersguide/screenwriting/download.html

documentaries, or in certain industries, such as film or television. *Motion picture screenwriters* usually write alone and exclusively for movies. *Television screenwriters* work very long hours in the studio. Many television shows have limited runs, so much of their work is not continuous.

Education and Training

In high school, you should develop your communication skills in English, theater, speech, and journalism classes. Social studies, foreign language, and history can also be helpful in creating intelligent scripts.

One important quality a screenwriter must have is a creative imagination and the ability to tell a story. The best way to prepare for a career as a screenwriter is to write and read every day. A college degree is not required, but a liberal arts education is helpful because it exposes you to a wide range of subjects. While in school, become involved in theater to learn about all of the required elements of a screenplay, such as character, plot, and theme. Book clubs, creative writing classes, and film study are also good ways to learn the basic elements of screenwriting.

Earnings

Annual wages for screenwriters vary widely. Some screenwriters make hundreds of thousands of dollars from their scripts.

Others write and film their own scripts without any payment at all, relying on backers and loans. Screenwriters who work independently do not earn regular salaries. They are paid a fee for each script they write. Those who write for ongoing television shows earn regular salaries. According to the Writers Guild of America (WGA), the median income for WGA members was $87,104 a year in 2001. Earnings ranged from less than $28,091 to more than $567,726.

Outlook

The job market for screenwriters, especially in television and film, is highly competitive because so many people are attracted to the field. In this industry, it is helpful to network and make contacts. In the creation of new television shows, and in motion picture screenwriting, persistence is important. On the brighter side, the growth of the cable television industry has increased demand for original screenplays and adaptations.

Books to Read

Blum, Richard. *Television and Screen Writing: From Concept to Contract.* 4th ed. Burlington, Mass.: Focal Press, 2000.

Brody, Larry. *Television Writing from the Inside Out: Your Channel to Success.* New York: Applause Books, 2003.

Flinn, Denny Martin. *How Not to Write a Screenplay: 101 Common Mistakes Most Screenwriters Make.* Los Angeles: Lone Eagle Publishing Company, 1999.

Goldberg, Lee, and William Rabkin. *Successful Television Writing.* Hoboken, N.J.: John Wiley & Sons, 2003.

Schellhardt, Laura, and John Logan. *Screenwriting For Dummies.* Hoboken, N.J.: John Wiley & Sons, 2003.

Smith, Evan. *Writing Television Sitcoms.* New York: Perigee Press, 1999.

FOR MORE INFO

To learn more about the television and film industries, to read interviews and articles by noted screenwriters, and to find links to many other screenwriting-related sites on the Internet, visit the WGA websites.

Writers Guild of America (WGA)

West Chapter

7000 West Third Street

Los Angeles, CA 90048

Tel: 800-548-4532

http://www.wga.org

Writers Guild of America (WGA)

East Chapter

555 West 57th Street, Suite 1230

New York, NY 10019

Tel: 212-767-7800

http://www.wgaeast.org

If you are thinking about becoming a screenwriter, you should also be open to careers in technical writing, journalism, or copywriting. Academic preparation in a related field may help you find another occupation in case you do not find a screenwriting job right away.

Sports Broadcasters and Announcers

What Sports Broadcasters and Announcers Do

Sports broadcasters, also called *sportscasters* or *sports anchors,* select, write, and deliver information about sports news on radio and television news broadcasts or provide announcements at sports events. They provide pre- and post-game coverage of sports events, as well as play-by-play coverage during the event.

The main job of sportscasters who work for news broadcasts is to summarize sports news and deliver daily sportscasts. Sportscasters who cover live events deliver a play-by-play report. The most common sports for which sportscasters deliver play-by-play broadcasts are baseball, basketball, football, hockey, and soccer. *Radio sportscasters* have to describe each play in enough detail that listeners can visualize the game. *Television sportscasters* comment on the players' actions, coaching decisions, technique, strategy, and other aspects of the game. Sportscasters provide game and player statistics and update them as the event progresses. They often interview coaches and athletes.

Stadium announcers provide spectators with public address announcements before and during a sports event. Stadium announcers may be sportscasters

Successful Sports Broadcasters and Announcers Have . . .

- ○ strong, pleasant speaking voices
- ○ excellent verbal and communication skills
- ○ good grammar and English usage
- ○ superior knowledge of sports
- ○ outgoing personalities
- ○ strong organizational skills
- ○ an ability to ad-lib, if necessary

or they may be professional announcers or emcees who make their living recording voice-overs for radio and television commercials, and for large corporations or department stores. Stadium announcers usually give the lineups for games, provide player names and numbers during specific times in a contest, make public announcements during timeouts and pauses in play, and generally keep the crowd involved in the event.

Education and Training

Take speech and English in high school to hone your communication skills. Participate in your favorite sports to get a knowledge of strategy, terminology, and rules and regulations. News sportscasters usually have a four-year college degree in communications or journalism. Personality and overall on-camera appearance may be more important to some employers than your level of education. If you are interested in a sports broadcasting career, learn all the details of a sport thoroughly. Make contacts with broadcasting professionals through internships and part-time or volunteer jobs.

Earnings

According to the Radio-Television News Directors Association (RTNDA), the average salaries of television sportscasters in 2001 ranged from

EXPLORING

○ Participate in a sport. By learning a sport inside and out, you learn the movements and techniques that you will be describing as a sportscaster.

○ Volunteer to help out with school teams by shagging balls, running drills, or managing equipment. Keeping statistics is good practice for learning percentages and background information on the strengths and weaknesses of each athlete.

○ Watch your favorite sports events on television without the sound. Tape-record your own play-by-play delivery.

○ Join your school's speech or debate team. Speaking before an audience can be the best practice for speaking in front of a camera or on a microphone.

○ Deejay on your school's radio station or volunteer at a local radio or cable television station.

○ Write about your school's sports teams for your school or local newspaper.

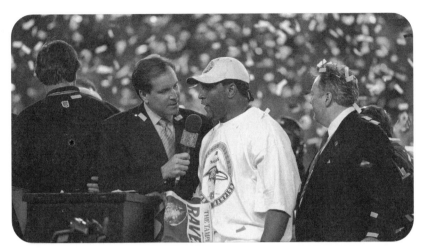

A sports broadcaster interviews Baltimore Ravens linebacker Ray Lewis after Superbowl XXXV. (Corbis)

$26,000 at the smallest stations to $121,000 at the largest ones. For all stations, the median salary was $35,000 a year.

Broadcasting on the Web

Check out these websites for examples of sports writing and sportscasting on the Internet. Most have audio sportscasts you can listen to.

ABC Sports
http://www.ABCsports.com

CNN/*Sports Illustrated*
http://sportsillustrated.cnn.com

ESPN
http://espn.go.com

Fox Sports
http://www.foxsports.com

Radio-Locator (links to more than 10,000 radio stations on the Internet)
http://www.radio-locator.com

FOR MORE INFO

For information about broadcast education and the broadcasting industry, contact
Broadcast Education Association
1771 N Street, NW
Washington, DC 20036-2891
Tel: 202-429-5354
Email: beainfo@beaweb.org
http://www.beaweb.org

To read answers to frequently asked questions about broadcasting, visit the NAB website.
National Association of Broadcasters (NAB)
1771 N Street, NW
Washington, DC 20036-2891
Tel: 202-429-5300
Email: nab@nab.org
http://www.nab.org

For industry information, contact
Radio-Television News Directors Association
1600 K Street, NW, Suite 700
Washington, DC 20006-2838
Tel: 202-659-6510
Email: rtnda@rtnda.org
http://www.rtnda.org

Top television sportscasters in major markets such as Chicago and New York can earn salaries that range from $100,000 to more than $1 million annually. Salaries are also usually higher for former athletes and recognized sports personalities or celebrities.

Sportscasting jobs in radio tend to pay less than those in television. The average salary for radio sportscasters in 2001, according to the RTNDA, was $29,500. Salaries ranged from $14,000 in the smallest markets to $50,000 in the largest markets.

Outlook

Competition for jobs in sportscasting will continue to be stiff. The better paying, larger market jobs will go to experienced sportscasters who can keep ratings high. Employment for sports broadcasters and announcers is expected to decline over the next decade. Not many new radio and television stations are expected to enter the market. Most of the job openings will come as sportscasters leave their jobs to retire, relocate, or enter other professions.

Talent Agents and Scouts

What Talent Agents and Scouts Do

An agent is a salesperson who sells artistic talent. *Talent agents* represent actors, directors, writers, models, and other people who work in television, film, radio, and theater. Agents promote their clients' talent and manage their legal contracts. Talent agents look for clients who have potential for success and then work aggressively to promote their clients to television and film directors, radio program directors, casting directors, production companies, and other potential employers.

Agents find clients in several ways. They review portfolios, screen tests, and audiotapes to evaluate potential clients' appearance, voice, personality, experience, ability to take direction, and other factors. Agents who work for an agency might be assigned a client by the agency, based on experience or a compatible personality. Some agents also work as *talent scouts* and actively search for new clients, whom they then bring to an agency. Or clients might approach agents who have good reputations and request their representation.

When an agent agrees to represent a client, they both sign a contract that specifies the extent of representation,

Successful Talent Agents and Scouts Are . . .

- good judges of talent
- tough negotiators
- hard working and aggressive
- detail-oriented and business-minded
- self-motivated
- ambitious
- excellent communicators

EXPLORING

○ Watch current television shows and movies to get a sense of the established and up-and-coming talents. Trace the careers of actors you like, including their early work in television shows, independent films, commercials, and stage work.

○ Contact a local talent agent to learn more about the career.

○ Volunteer or intern at a talent agency to find out more about the career.

the time period, payment, and other legal considerations.

Agents also work closely with the potential employers of their clients. They need to satisfy the needs of both parties. Agents who represent actors have a network of directors, producers, advertising executives, and photographers that they contact frequently to see if any of their clients can meet their needs.

When agents see a possible match between employer and client, they speak to both and quickly organize meetings, interviews, or auditions. Agents must be persistent and aggressive on behalf of their clients. They spend time on the phone with employers, convincing them of their clients' talents and persuading them to hire clients.

When an employer agrees to hire a client, the agent helps negotiate a contract that outlines salary, benefits, promotional appearances, and other fees, rights, and obligations. Agents have to look out for the best interests of their clients and at the same time satisfy employers in order to establish continuing, long-lasting relationships.

The largest talent agencies are located in Los Angeles and New York City, where the television and film industries are centered. Independent agents have offices throughout the country.

Education and Training

In high school, you should take courses in business, mathematics, and accounting to prepare for the management aspects of an agent's job. Take English and speech courses to develop good communication skills because you will need to be a good negotiator. You also need a good eye for talent, so be sure to develop some expertise in television, radio, film, and related areas.

Although some agents receive their training on the job, a bachelor's degree is strongly recommended for work in this field. Advanced degrees in law and business are becoming increasingly popular since talent agents must write contracts according to legal regulations.

Earnings

Earnings for agents vary greatly, depending on the success of the agent and his or her clients. An agency typically receives 10 to 15 percent of a client's fee for a project. An agent is then paid a commission by the agency as well as a base salary. Assistants generally make entry-level salaries of between $18,000 and $20,000 a year. In the first few years, an agent will make between $25,000 and $50,000 a year. However, those working for the top agencies can make much more. Working for an agency, an experienced agent will receive health and retirement benefits, bonuses, and paid travel and accommodations.

Industry Publications

- ○ *Daily Variety* (http://www.variety.com)
- ○ *Entertainment Weekly* (http://www.ew.com)
- ○ *The Hollywood Reporter* (http://www.hollywoodreporter. com)
- ○ *Premiere* (http://www.premiere.com)
- ○ *Radio & Records* (http://www.radioandrecords.com)

FOR MORE INFO

For general information on management careers in the performing arts, contact
North American Performing Arts Managers and Agents
459 Columbus Avenue, Suite 133
New York, NY 10024
Email: info@napama.org
http://www.napama.org

Visit the SAG website for information about acting in television and films and for a list of talent agencies.
Screen Actors Guild (SAG)
5757 Wilshire Boulevard
Los Angeles, CA 90036-3600
http://www.sag.com

Outlook

Although the television and film industries have expanded greatly in recent years, competition for positions as talent agents and scouts is very intense. It may take years and years to become successful in the field, and some aspiring agents never make it in the business. On the plus side, overseas markets for U.S. television shows and films are expanding, so even programs and motion pictures that don't do so well domestically can still turn a tidy profit. Also, more original cable television programming will lead to more actors and performers seeking representation. These expanding markets should create steady opportunities for the most experienced talent agents and scouts. Little growth is expected in the radio industry over the next several years. Talent agents and scouts who focus on representing clients in this industry will enjoy average employment prospects over the next decade.

Television Directors

What Television Directors Do

Television directors coordinate the making of television shows, commercials, music videos, and other productions. They work with actors, costume designers, camera operators, lighting designers, and producers. Directors are involved in every stage from hiring actors to editing the final show. Many television directors also work in the motion picture industry. Others work on industrial films and travelogues.

Producers are in charge of the business and financial side of a television or film project. *Directors* are in charge of the creative and technical side. Usually a producer hires the director, but they work closely together. They plan a budget and production schedule, including time for research, filming, and editing.

Directors work with the scriptwriter, actors, studio technicians, and set designers. They give directions to many different people. They choose costumes, scenery, and music. During rehearsals they plan the action carefully, telling actors how to move and interpret the script. They coach the actors to help them give their best performances. At the same time, directors give directions for sets and lighting and decide on the order and angles of camera shots. Once filming is finished, they supervise editing and add sound and special effects.

Successful Television Directors Are . . .

- artistic
- strong leaders
- excellent time managers
- able to work well under deadline pressure
- decisive
- self-confident
- able to work with many different types of people

Some television directors work on regular shows or series, such as soap operas, situation comedies, sporting events, talk shows, and game shows. These directors work on-set or at a console with a row of television monitors. The monitors show what is going on in different parts of the studio from different camera angles.

Television directors work on a variety of productions. For example, they may direct local news programs and national sporting events or tape commercials for businesses. And with the development of "narrowcasting" (broadcasting meant for limited viewing, such as for classrooms, hospitals, or corporations), some directors create programming for very small audiences.

EXPLORING

○ Study your favorite television shows to see what makes them interesting.

○ If your high school has its own television station, join the production crew.

○ Get involved with your school's drama club and participate in plays.

○ Tour a local television news studio to learn more about the field.

○ Many camps and workshops offer programs for students interested in film work. For example, the University of Wisconsin offers its Summer Art Studio for students in grades six through 12. Visit http://www.uwgb.edu/outreach/camps.

Education and Training

You can start now to prepare for a career in directing. Take English literature classes to learn storytelling techniques. Theater classes will teach you about acting. Photography courses can teach you about visual composition.

Even though there are no specific requirements for becoming a director, the most successful ones have a wide variety of talents and experience, as well as good business and management skills. You must be able to develop ideas and be good at communicating with others.

Many colleges and universities offer film majors with concentration in directing. These programs require you to direct your own films. They also offer internships and other practical learning experiences. The Directors Guild of America offers an Assistant

Books to Read

Bare, Richard L., and James Garner. *The Film Director: Updated for Today's Filmmaker, the Classic, Practical Reference to Motion Picture and Television Techniques.* New York: John Wiley & Sons, 2000.

Brooks, Tim, and Earle F. Marsh. *The Complete Directory to Prime Time Network and Cable TV Shows: 1946–Present.* New York: Ballantine Books, 2003.

Hill, Tom. *TV Land To Go: The Big Books of TV Lists, TV Lore, and TV Bests.* New York: Fireside, 2001.

O'Brien, Lisa. *Lights, Camera, Action!: Making Movies and TV from the Inside Out.* Toronto: Maple Tree Press, 1998.

Directors Training Program for those who have a bachelor's degree or two years of experience in television or movie production. (See For More Info.)

Many directors begin at small television stations or community theaters or as production assistants for films. Many directors have worked for a number of years as actors, or in some other capacity within the industry, to gain experience.

Earnings

Salaries for television directors vary greatly based on the type of programs that they direct. Directors of television shows are paid by the type of show. For example, directors of soap operas can earn $2,000 per episode. Television news directors earned salaries that ranged from $18,000 to $250,000 in 2001, according to a survey by the Radio-Television News Directors Association. The U.S. Department of Labor reports that television directors employed in all areas of the industry had median earnings of $47,490 in 2002.

Directors who work full time for television stations or other organizations generally receive benefits such as health insurance and paid vacation and sick days. Directors who work on a freelance basis do not receive paid sick and vacation days and are responsible for paying their own health insurance costs.

Outlook

Because of the growth of the cable television and video- and DVD-rental industries, the employment outlook for directors is good. Employment should grow about as fast as the average over the next decade. However, many people are interested in becoming directors and there will be stiff competition for jobs.

FOR MORE INFO

For information on the film and television industries, visit the AFI website.
American Film Institute (AFI)
2021 North Western Avenue
Los Angeles, CA 90027-1657
Tel: 323-856-7600
http://afionline.org

For information about broadcast education and the broadcasting industry, contact
Broadcast Education Association
1771 N Street, NW
Washington, DC 20036-2891
Tel: 202-429-5354
Email: beainfo@beaweb.org
http://www.beaweb.org

For information about the Assistant Directors Training Program, contact
Directors Guild of America
7920 Sunset Boulevard
Los Angeles, CA 90046

Tel: 310-289-2000
http://www.dga.org

For industry information, contact
Radio-Television News Directors Association
1600 K Street, NW, Suite 700
Washington, DC 20006-2838
Tel: 202-659-6510
Email: rtnda@rtnda.org
http://www.rtnda.org

For information on the Emmy Awards and to read about members of its Hall of Fame, visit the ATAS website.
Academy of Television Arts and Sciences (ATAS)
http://www.emmys.org

This website contains links to numerous television-related sites and lists colleges and universities worldwide that offer training in television broadcast production.
CineMedia
http://www.cinemedia.org

Television Editors

What Television Editors Do

Television editors perform an important role in the creation of television shows, commercials, and videos. They use special equipment to alter an unedited movie or videotape and arrange the material to create the most effective product possible. Television editors edit sitcoms, dramas, documentaries, commercials, footage for newscasts, made-for-TV movies, music videos, and other television programming. Television editors may also be employed in the film industry.

Television editors work with producers and directors from the earliest phases of shooting and production. Editors learn about the objectives of the television show from producers. The producer may explain the larger scope of the project so that the editor knows the best way to approach the work when it is time to edit the videotape or film. With the director, editors discuss the objective and story line of the film or video. They may discuss scenes and camera angles before filming even begins so that the editor understands the director's vision for the final piece.

Once filming is complete, television editors rate and choose the segments that will be used. Sometimes there are five or 10 takes of one scene, and editors select segments based on video or film quality, dramatic value, or other criteria. Editors refer to the script and the director's notes when making

Try It!

Visit the DigiPuppet website to view and edit two scenes of actual film footage. (Note: You will need one of the following home computer editing programs: iMovie 4, Final Cut Pro, Final Cut Express 2, Adobe Premiere 4.2, or Avid Free DV.)

Digital Puppet
http://www.digipuppet.com

A group of editors sits at a control board to edit programming. (Corbis)

their choices. They time the video or film segments to specified lengths and reassemble the segments in a sequence that has the greatest effect and makes the most sense. Editors and directors review the reassembled material on a video monitor. Editors then make further adjustments and corrections until the director and producer are satisfied.

Film editors use nonlinear processes more often. In this process, the video or film is transferred to a digital format. A computer database tracks individual frames and puts all the scenes together in a folder of information. This information is stored on a computer hard drive and can be brought up instantly on a screen, allowing the editor to access scenes and frames with the click of a mouse.

Sound editors work on television and film soundtracks. They often keep libraries of sounds that they frequently use for various projects, including natural sounds such as thunder or raindrops, animal noises, motor sounds, or musical interludes. Some sound editors specialize in music, and others work with sound effects. They may use unusual objects, machines, or computer-generated noisemakers to create a desired sound for a television show or film.

Education and Training

Television editing requires a creative perspective along with technical skills. Thus, you should take English, speech, theater, art, photography, and other courses that will allow you to develop writing skills. If your high school offers classes in either film history or film production, be sure to take those courses.

Training to work as a television editor takes many years. The best educational background is in the liberal arts. Some employers require a bachelor's degree for those seeking positions as editors. English, journalism, theater, or film editing are good majors

Books to Read

Dancyger, Ken. *The Technique of Film and Video Editing: History, Theory, and Practice.* Burlington, Mass.: Focal Press, 2002.

Goodman, Robert M., and Patrick McGrath. *Editing Digital Video: The Complete Creative and Technical Guide.* New York: McGraw-Hill, 2002.

Hollyn, Norman. *The Film Editing Room Handbook: How to Manage the Near Chaos of the Cutting Room.* Los Angeles: Lone Eagle Publishing Company, 1999.

to pursue. Some community and two-year colleges offer film study programs with courses in film and video editing. Universities with departments of broadcast journalism offer courses in film and video editing and also may have contacts at local television stations.

Much of the day-to-day work of television editors can be learned in an apprenticeship. By working closely with an editor, an apprentice can learn specific film-editing techniques.

Earnings

Television editors are not as highly paid as film editors or other film and television industry professionals. However, television editors have more authority in the production of a project than many other industry workers. According to the U.S. Department of Labor, the median annual wage for television editors was $38,410 in 2002. Some television editors earn less than $20,000 a year, while some earn more than $78,000. The most experienced and sought-after television editors command much higher salaries.

EXPLORING

- ○ Join a film or video club at your school or community center.
- ○ Research different kinds of television projects, including sitcoms, news shows, dramas, commercials, music videos, and documentaries.
- ○ Experiment with one of the many digital film editing systems available for home computers. You can download your own digital video into your computer, edit the material, and then add your own special effects and titles.
- ○ Volunteer at a local television station and observe editors and other professionals at work.

Outlook

Employment of television editors is expected to grow about as fast as the average in the next decade. The growth of cable television and the emergence of the Internet as a venue for artistic productions will increase the demand for editors.

The digital revolution will greatly affect the editing process. Editors will work much more closely with special effects experts in putting together projects. Digital technology may allow some prospective editors more direct routes into the industry, but the majority of editors will have to follow traditional routes, obtaining years of experience before being considered for top jobs.

FOR MORE INFO

The ACE features career and education information for film editors on its Web page, as well as information about internship opportunities and sample articles from Cinemeditor *magazine.*

American Cinema Editors (ACE)
100 Universal City Plaza
Building 2282, Room 234
Universal City, CA 91608
Tel: 818-777-2900
Email: amercinema@earthlink.net
http://www.ace-filmeditors.org

For information about AFI's Conservatory's master of fine arts in editing and to read interviews with professionals, visit the AFI website.

American Film Institute (AFI)
2021 North Western Avenue
Los Angeles, CA 90027
Tel: 323-856-7600
http://www.afi.com

For information on the Emmy Awards and to read about members of its Hall of Fame, visit the ATAS website:

Academy of Television Arts and Sciences (ATAS)
http://www.emmys.org

This website contains links to numerous television-related sites and lists colleges and universities worldwide that offer training in television broadcast production.

CineMedia
http://www.cinemedia.org

Television Producers

What Television Producers Do

Television producers are behind-the-scenes professionals who are involved with budgeting and financing, working out a production time line, casting appropriate actors, or even hiring the crew for a TV program. Because of the varied nature of television programming, a producer's role may also change from project to project. A producer on one project, for example, may only be involved in arranging financial backing and putting together the creative team of directors and actors. A producer on another project may oversee every detail of the production, including arranging for equipment and scheduling personnel. Many producers also work in the film industry.

Television producers work as *independent producers,* often known as *freelance producers,* or they are employed by television networks, stations, and production companies. One of the main responsibilities of independent producers (those with their own production companies) may be to raise money for projects. A producer employed by a television station, on the other hand, may be given a budget to work with. In either case, the producer is responsible for keeping an eye on costs and making sure the project stays within budget. This also requires time-management skills,

To Be a Successful Television Producer, You Should . . .

- ○ be organized
- ○ have excellent communication skills
- ○ be self-confident
- ○ have knowledge of the television industry
- ○ be able to manage others
- ○ have business and financial expertise
- ○ be creative and able to solve problems quickly
- ○ be willing to travel to shooting locations, if necessary

A television producer for ABC's World News Tonight *meets with anchorman Peter Jennings.* (Corbis)

because the producer must schedule just the right amount of time for different phases of production. If the producer underestimates the time needed for filming on location, for example, the producer's company will need to pay the expenses for extra time on location, causing the project to go over budget.

A producer's responsibilities are also affected by what type of project he or she works on. For example, *newscast producers,* along with reporters, determine what stories are worth broadcasting. Newscast producers assign stories, review taped reports, and may even help edit the material. Often these producers must deal with late-breaking developments and must quickly assign reporters and TV crews to cover a story, then weave the new report into the broadcast while staying within the broadcast's time requirements. The newscast is a combination of live and taped segments, and the producer often needs to make decisions quickly while the show is on the air.

Television Firsts

1923 First TV camera and TV tube were patented by Vladimir K. Zworykin
1927 First electronic image telecast
1928 First dramatic program, *The Queen's Messenger,* broadcast to four television sets
1941 First commercial, a 10-second spot for Bulova watches, debuts
1954 First coast-to-coast colorcast (*Tournament of Roses Parade*) broadcast
1955 First wireless remote control, Zenith's "Flash-matic," introduced
1972 First cable network, Home Box Office, debuts
1998 First digital television broadcast

Documentary producers are also very actively involved in their productions, but they typically have days, rather than hours, to complete projects. They may be involved in deciding on a concept for the documentary; hiring writers, directors, and the crew; and scouting out locations and finding interview subjects. Once interviews and other segments are taped, they may review the material, select the best footage, and edit it into a program of predetermined length.

Whereas newscast and documentary producers rely on their news judgment, *drama and comedy producers* rely on their understanding of the entertainment world. These producers come up with ideas for shows; hire writers, directors, and actors; and review the final product for its tone and content.

EXPLORING

○ Join a film or video club at your school or in your community.
○ Get involved in your school's theater productions, especially in a fund-raising capacity
○ Volunteer to work on committees that organize, produce, and publicize special events at your school or religious center.
○ Ask your teacher to set up an informational interview with a local producer. Ask the producer the following questions: What type of educational background do you have? What is the hardest part of your job? What is the most enjoyable part? What advice can you give me on how to best prepare for this career?

Education and Training

In high school, English composition and speech courses will help you develop writing and communication skills. Business and economics courses can prepare you for the financial responsibilities of a producer's job.

Many television producers have earned college degrees in broadcast journalism or film. However, experience is often the best qualification for this job. Most producers work their way into the position from other television-related jobs, such as production, acting, editing, and directing. It is important to have contacts in the industry and with potential investors.

FOR MORE INFO

For film news and information on educational programs, visit the AFI website.

American Film Institute (AFI)
2021 North Western Avenue
Los Angeles, CA 90027-1657
Tel: 323-856-7600
Email: info@afionline.org
http://www.afi.com

For answers to frequently asked questions about production careers, visit the PGA website.

Producers Guild of America (PGA)
8530 Wilshire Boulevard, Suite 450
Beverly Hills, CA 90211
Tel: 310-358-9020
Email: info@producersguild.org
http://www.producersguild.org

Earnings

Film producers are generally paid a percentage of the project's profits or a fee negotiated between the producer and a studio. The U.S. Department of Labor reports that television producers earned median salaries of $38,480 in 2002. Salaries for all producers ranged from less than $23,300 to more than $119,760. Producers of highly successful films can earn $200,000 or more, while those who make low-budget films might earn considerably less than the average. Newscast executive producers earned salaries that ranged from $18,000 to $115,000 in 2001, according to the Radio-Television News Directors Association.

Outlook

Employment for television producers is expected to grow about as fast as the average in the coming years. Opportunities may increase with the expansion of cable and satellite television, the growing popularity of video and DVD rentals, and an increased overseas demand for American-made programming, but competition for jobs will be strong. Live theater and entertainment will also provide job openings.

Weather Forecasters

What Weather Forecasters Do

Weather forecasters compile and analyze weather information and prepare reports for daily and nightly television or radio newscasts. Forecasters, also known as *broadcast meteorologists* and *weathercasters*, create graphics, write scripts, and explain weather maps to audiences. They also provide special reports during extreme weather conditions and predict future weather patterns. To make accurate forecasts, forecasters may conduct research on such subjects as atmospheric electricity, clouds, precipitation, hurricanes, and data collected from weather satellites. Other areas of research used to forecast weather may include ocean currents and temperature.

In addition to broadcasting weather reports, TV and radio weather forecasters often visit schools and community centers to speak on weather safety. They are also frequently involved in broadcast station promotions, taking part in community events.

Education and Training

In high school, you can prepare for a career as a weather forecaster by taking a number of different classes. Concentrate on the sciences—earth science, biology, chemistry, and physics—to give you an understanding of the environment and how dif-

To Be a Successful Weather Forecaster, You Should . . .

○ have a passion for the weather and other environmental topics
○ be able to work well under pressure
○ be able to communicate weather situations and terms easily to your audience
○ have a willingness to work long hours during major weather events such as snowstorms, hurricanes, tornadoes, floods, and heat waves

ferent elements interact. Geography and mathematics courses will also be useful. Take computer classes to familiarize yourself with computers and gain experience working with graphics programs. Take plenty of English and speech classes. As a broadcaster, you will need to have excellent writing and speaking skills. If your school offers any media courses in which you learn how to broadcast a radio or television show, be sure to take those classes.

EXPLORING

○ Keep a journal of weather activity in your area.
○ Visit The Weather Channel (http://www.weather.com) and other weather-related websites
○ Watch weather forecasters on television. Determine what you like and dislike about each forecaster's presentation.
○ Join a science or weather club in your school or your community.
○ Ask a teacher or guidance counselor to schedule a trip to a local television or radio station so you can watch weather forecasters in action.
○ Volunteer to work at your school's radio or TV station. If your school doesn't have one of these stations, join the newspaper staff to get some experience working with the media.

Although a degree in meteorology or atmospheric science is not required to become a weather forecaster, it is necessary for advancement. While in college, you should also continue to take English, speech, and communications classes to hone your communication skills and computer classes to keep up to date with this technology. It is also important to complete an internship as a student weather forecaster with a TV or radio station.

Earnings

Salaries for weather forecasters vary greatly according to level of experience, the region in which they work, and type of employer. Weather forecasters who are employed by the television industry typically earn more than those working in radio. According to a salary survey by the Radio-Television News Directors Association, television weathercasters earned salaries that ranged from

Who Employs Weather Forecasters?

- television stations
- radio stations
- cable networks such as The Weather Channel
- private weather consulting firms
- airlines
- corporations
- U.S. military
- National Weather Service
- National Oceanic and Atmospheric Administration
- U.S. Department of Agriculture
- U.S. Department of Defense
- other government agencies

$16,000 to $1,000,000 in 2001, with a median of $43,800. Radio weathercasters in small markets may earn less than these amounts.

According to the U.S. Department of Labor, salaries for all atmospheric scientists (including weather forecasters) ranged from less than $30,220 to more than $92,430 in 2002.

Outlook

The U.S. Department of Labor predicts that employment for all atmospheric scientists will increase about as fast as the average over the next decade. However, the department also predicts that employment for television and radio announcers will decline during the same time period. Usually, meteorologists are able to find work in the field upon graduation, though they may have to be flexible about the area of meteorology and region of the country in which they work. Positions for broadcast meteorologists, as with any positions in broadcast news, are in high demand. The number of news departments and news staffs is not expected to grow in the next decade, and the growing number of graduates looking for work in news departments will make this field very competitive.

FOR MORE INFO

Visit the AMS website for a list of colleges offering meteorology programs and to read A Career Guide for the Atmospheric Sciences.
American Meteorological Society (AMS)
45 Beacon Street
Boston, MA 02108-3693
Tel: 617-227-2425
Email: amsinfo@ametsoc.org
http://www.ametsoc.org/ams

For weather and employment information and links to other weather-related sites, visit the NOAA website.
National Oceanic and Atmospheric Administration (NOAA)
14th Street and Constitution Avenue, NW, Room 6217
Washington, DC 20230
Tel: 202-482-6090
Email: noaa-outreach@noaa.gov
http://www.noaa.gov

For a list of schools with degree programs in meteorology or atmospheric science, visit the NWA website.
National Weather Association (NWA)
1697 Capri Way
Charlottesville, VA 22911-3534
Tel: 434-296-9966
Email: NatWeaAsoc@aol.com
http://www.nwas.org

To learn more about the weather, visit the NWS website.
National Weather Service (NWS)
1325 East-West Highway
Silver Spring, MD 20910
http://www.nws.noaa.gov

This website, presented by the University of Illinois, provides an overview of meteorology for high school and undergraduate students.
WW2010
http://ww2010.atmos.uiuc.edu

Glossary

accredited   approved as meeting established standards for providing good training and education; this approval is usually given to a school or a program in a school by an independent organization of professionals

apprentice   person who is learning a trade by working under the supervision of a skilled worker; apprentices often receive classroom instruction in addition to their supervised practical experience

associate's degree   academic rank or title granted by a community or junior college or similar institution to graduates of a two-year program of education beyond high school

bachelor's degree   academic rank or title given to a person who has completed a four-year program of study at a college or university; also called an undergraduate degree or baccalaureate

career   occupation for which a worker receives training and has an opportunity for advancement

certified   approved as meeting established requirements for skill, knowledge, and experience in a particular field; people are certified by the organization of professionals in their field

college   higher education institution that is above the high school level

community college   public two-year college attended by students who do not usually live at the college; a graduate of a community college receives an associate's degree and may transfer to a four-year college or university to complete a bachelor's degree

diploma   certificate or document given by a school to show that a person has completed a course or has graduated from the school

distance education   type of educational program that allows students to take classes and complete their education by mail or the Internet

doctorate   highest academic rank or title granted by a graduate school to a person who has completed a two- to three-year program after having received a master's degree

fringe benefit   payment or benefit to an employee in addition to regular wages or salary; examples of fringe benefits include a pension, a paid vacation, and health or life insurance

graduate school   school that people may attend after they have received their bachelor's degree; people who complete an educational program at a graduate school earn a master's degree or a doctorate

intern   advanced student (usually one with at least some college training) who is employed in a job that is intended to provide supervised practical career experience

internship   (1) the position or job of an intern; (2) period of time when a person is an intern

junior college   two-year college that offers courses like those in the first half of a four-year college program; graduates of a junior college usually receive an associate's degree and may transfer to a four-year college or university to complete a bachelor's degree

liberal arts   subjects covered by college courses that develop broad general knowledge rather than specific occupational skills; the liberal arts are often considered to include philosophy, literature and the arts, history, language, and some courses in the social sciences and natural sciences

major (in college)   academic field in which a student specializes and receives a degree

master's degree academic rank or title granted by a graduate school to a person who has completed a one- or two-year program after having received a bachelor's degree

online education academic study that is performed by using a computer and the Internet

pension amount of money paid regularly by an employer to a former employee after he or she retires from working

scholarship gift of money to a student to help the student pay for further education

social studies courses of study (such as civics, geography, and history) that deal with how human societies work

starting salary salary paid to a newly hired employee; the starting salary is usually a smaller amount than is paid to a more experienced worker

technical college private or public college offering two- or four-year programs in technical subjects; technical colleges offer courses in both general and technical subjects and award associate's degrees and bachelor's degrees

undergraduate student at a college or university who has not yet received a degree

undergraduate degree see **bachelor's degree**

union organization whose members are workers in a particular industry or company; the union works to gain better wages, benefits, and working conditions for its members; also called a labor union or trade union

wage money that is paid in return for work done, especially money paid on the basis of the number of hours or days worked

Index of Job Titles

Browse and Learn More

Books

Albarran, Alan B., and Gregory G. Pitts. *The Radio Broadcasting Industry*. Allyn & Bacon Series in Mass Communication. Boston: Pearson Allyn & Bacon, 2001.

Crouch, Tanja L. *100 Careers in Film and Television*. Hauppauge, N.Y.: Barrons Educational Series, 2003.

Ellis, Elmo Israel. *Opportunities in Broadcasting Careers*. New York: McGraw-Hill, 1999.

Field, Shelly, and Chris Scherer. *Career Opportunities in Radio*. New York: Facts On File, 2004.

Gordon, Sandra. *Action!: Establishing Your Career in Film and Television Production*. Milwaukee, Wisc.: Hal Leonard Corporation, 2002.

Keith, Michael C. *The Radio Station*. 6th ed. Burlington, Mass.: Focal Press, 2004.

Somervill, Barbara A. *Backstage at a Newscast*. High Interest Books: Backstage Pass. New York: Children's Press, 2003.

Websites

About.com: Radio
http://radio.about.com

Federal Communications Commission
http://www.fcc.gov

History of Radio
http://history.acusd.edu/gen/recording/radio.html

Museum of Broadcast Communications

http://www.museum.tv

National Association of Broadcasters

http://www.nab.org

National Public Radio

http://www.npr.org

Radio Hall of Fame

http://www.radiohof.org

Television History: The First 75 Years

http://www.tvhistory.tv

Yahoo!: Radio

http://dir.yahoo.com/News_and_Media/Radio

Yahoo!: Television

http://dir.yahoo.com/News_and_Media/Television